Hart County #1

HER
SECRET

Center Point
Large Print

Also by Shelley Shepard Gray and available from Center Point Large Print:

Proposal at Siesta Key
Loyal Heart
Amish Family Christmas

Also by Shelley Gray and available from Center Point Large Print:

Deception on Sable Hill

HER SECRET

THE AMISH OF HART COUNTY

Shelley Shepard Gray

CENTER POINT LARGE PRINT
THORNDIKE, MAINE

This Center Point Large Print edition is published
in the year 2017 by arrangement with Avon Inspire,
an imprint of HarperCollins Publishers.

The text of this Large Print edition is unabridged.
In other aspects, this book may vary
from the original edition.
Printed in the United States of America
on permanent paper.
Set in 16-point Times New Roman type.

ISBN: 978-1-68324-405-9

Library of Congress Cataloging-in-Publication Data

Names: Gray, Shelley Shepard, author.
Title: Her secret : the Amish of hart country / Shelley Shepard Gray.
Description: Center Point Large Print edition. | Thorndike, Maine :
Center Point Large Print, 2017.
Identifiers: LCCN 2017009426 | ISBN 9781683244059
    (hardcover : alk. paper)
Subjects: LCSH: Amish—Fiction. | Large type books. | GSAFD:
Mystery fiction.
Classification: LCC PS3607.R3966 H47 2017 | DDC 813/.6—dc23
LC record available at https://lccn.loc.gov/2017009426

To Nicole Resciniti. My agent and my friend.
Thank you for being there for me in
immeasurable ways. Thank you, also,
for encouraging me to still have big dreams.
I'm indebted to you.

How do you know what your life will be like tomorrow? Your life is like the morning fog—it's here a little while, then it's gone.

JAMES 4:14

Rare indeed is the person who looks for trouble and fails to find it.

AMISH PROVERB

Prologue

"This just arrived for you, Hannah."

Hannah Hilty looked up from the table she was clearing to see her manager by the reception desk at the Berlin Country Store. Blowing a wisp of hair off her brow, and wiping her hands on the dish towel tucked in the sash of her apron, Hannah hurried to take the brown envelope out of Kennedy Frazier's hands.

"*Danke*," she said politely. "I'm not sure why someone would have given you an envelope for me, though."

"Actually, someone slipped it through our mail slot. In any case, I was happy to hold on to it for you." She winked. "I'm glad you were working today. Otherwise, I would have had to remember to hand it to you for your next shift."

"Oh, you would have remembered . . . eventually." If there was one thing Hannah had learned about her manager, it was that Kennedy sometimes bit off more than she could chew. Because of that, she was a bit of a scatterbrain.

"You're right. One day I am going to become more organized and learn to say no, too,"

Kennedy quipped before greeting the couple who had just walked into the quaint restaurant.

Seeing that Kennedy was taking the couple to another girl's station to be seated, Hannah took advantage of the moment to stand over to the side and examine the envelope.

She had no idea what could be inside. Maybe it was the information about the latest library reading schedule? She'd recently started volunteering to read to preschoolers twice a week. Or, it could possibly be a brochure about the latest Pioneer bus schedule for trips to Pinecraft. She and Kirsten had always yearned to head down to Pinecraft one winter. Now that she was twenty, her parents had at last given permission for her to go.

Thinking that sending a brochure to her this way was something that Kirsten would definitely do, Hannah tore open the top and pulled out the contents.

Then froze.

Scrawled at the top of a piece of notebook paper were four words:

You are mine, Hannah

Attached to it were four black-and-white photos, each one of her. Her hands began to shake.

There she was, walking to work, her shawl half covering her white *kapp* and shoulders. Another showed her laughing with Kirsten on the steps of the library. The third was a picture of her and her little brother, Ben, outside the Amish school.

The last was the most disturbing of all. It was a silhouette of Hannah's body in front of her window. Her curtains were closed, of course, but they might as well have been wide open, given that it had been taken at night and the light from her kerosene lantern had illuminated her in detail. It was obvious that she was only partly dressed and her hair was loose. She'd been changing into her nightgown.

Hannah felt sick to her stomach.

Trent had been following her around and taking pictures of her.

It was disturbing enough, since the Amish didn't like their pictures taken. Everyone knew that, especially Trent. Though he was English, he'd lived in Berlin all his life.

He'd also pursued her for the last two years. For a short period of time, they'd even been friends. Once, she'd even considered returning his affection. It had been at the height of her *rumspringa*, and she'd been mighty foolish.

Thinking back to that time, when she'd been so eager to prove to herself and her parents that she was mature and independent, she'd made a lot of mistakes. Encouraging Trent had been her worst one.

But after careful prayer and taking the time to really consider the consequences of her actions, she'd quietly told Trent that they could only ever be friends.

He hadn't accepted her decision easily.

Actually, he'd been upset and had refused to give credence to her reasons.

Then he'd begun seeking her out in earnest. He would be on the street when she walked, at the market when she went shopping. He'd begun to send her bouquets of daisies, too.

Now, looking at the pictures, seeing his note, Hannah realized that his infatuation had turned into something disturbing. *Nee*, it was more than that.

He had frightened her.

"Hannah? Hannah!" Kennedy said as she hurried over to her side. "What's wrong? Oh my word, you are looking as white as a sheet. What was in the envelope?"

"This."

Kennedy took hold of the pictures. "What are these? Oh, my . . . someone sent you photos of yourself? Who would do that?" she mused. "Everyone knows . . ." Her voice drifted off as she flipped through the pictures. "Hannah!"

"I know." Realizing that she was no doubt shaking like a leaf, she said, "I don't know what I'm gonna do."

"I do," Kennedy said, resolve thick in her voice. "You are going to go right home and show your parents. Something has to be done about this."

Hannah agreed. Something did need to be done, though whether or not it would make a difference was anyone's guess. So far, everything she'd tried to do to dissuade Trent had been ignored.

Worse, it was becoming apparent that he was going to continue to terrorize her no matter what she did or said. Actually, she was fairly certain his actions were only going to get worse.

Chapter 1

Three months later
July 9
Munfordville, Kentucky

"Go on, now, Hannah," her mother prodded with a touch of impatience in her voice. "Go take a walk like you used to do. It will do you a world of good."

Staring at the front door with its two deadbolts and security chain, Hannah hesitated. That door symbolized both her safety and her worst fears. Sometimes, she didn't even want to touch the heavy oak, let alone the pewter-colored handle.

From the moment she'd seen those pictures of herself three months ago, she'd mentally locked herself down. Fearing what others were doing no longer felt like overreacting. Instead, it felt safe.

But going outside would also give her some

relief from the confines of her house. And, well, she could admit it—a walk also gave her a welcome respite from her annoying brother and sister. They were teenagers and seemed to thrive on being self-centered.

Walking up behind her, her mother placed the palms of her hands on Hannah's shoulders and rested her chin lightly on the top of Hannah's head. She'd done this for as long as Hannah could remember. When she was a little girl, it would make her giggle. She'd thought it was funny that her mother was able to rest her chin on her head without wrinkling the top of her *kapp*.

Later, when she was eleven and twelve, it used to make Hannah feel self-conscious about how petite she was. When she was fifteen, she'd hated her mother's need to be so protective. She'd yearned for experiences, not confining hugs.

But now, she rather enjoyed feeling her mother's warm hands on her shoulders and chin on her head. It made her feel secure. It was also a welcome reminder that her mother loved her dearly.

But even that comforting touch couldn't take away the feeling that someone was always watching her whenever she was out in the open. It didn't seem to matter that her parents were sure that Trent didn't know where they'd moved to.

No matter how hard Hannah tried, she couldn't seem to escape the feeling that she was in danger.

• • •

"Today ain't a good day, Mamm," she said in a rush. "It's cloudy out. It might rain. Plus, it looks a little chilly, too. Maybe I'll go tomorrow."

"Today is a fine day. It is a bit on the cool side for July, but it's sunny. If you put on a sweater, you won't notice the cool temperature at all."

It did look pretty out, but weather was the last thing she was concerned about. And because she didn't want to try to explain her irrational fears all over again, she used her brother and sister as her excuse. "I told Ben and Jenny that I would help them with their assignments. I should probably do that." Not that they would want to listen to her. These days, her younger siblings didn't seem to want to listen to much of anything. Hannah feared they were both running wild.

"Hannah, dear. You know I love all of my *kinner*. However, even the best person in the world would need a break from Ben and Jenny from time to time. You need a break, *jah*?"

"Maybe," she mumbled as she turned to face her.

"I know so," Mamm corrected, her hazel-colored eyes full of mirth. "They surely are a handful right now."

"They are selfish and difficult, Mamm," Hannah said before she could stop herself. "They also are in perpetually bad moods."

Mamm laughed. "They are thirteen and fourteen, child. Each on the cusp of discovering who they are."

Thinking of how both of them blamed Hannah for their unhappiness and were not shy about sharing their feelings, Hannah groaned. "It's more than that."

Lines of worry appeared at the corners of her eyes. "I wouldn't say they are quite that bad, though I know they've been a trial to you. But just like their difficulties will one day fade, your fears will, too . . . if you allow them."

"If I allow them?"

"Dear, one day this, too, shall pass."

This, too, shall pass. It was her mother's favorite saying. Even though it didn't come from the Bible, Hannah thought it was certainly helpful to remember. Hannah felt like it was beginning to have some rejuvenating effects on her as well.

Ever since she'd run home with that envelope full of photographs, Hannah had been waiting for this awful time in her life to pass. Her parents had taken her worries seriously, especially since it was not the first time Trent had taken a photo of her or made her feel uncomfortable.

It hadn't even been the fourth or fifth time.

He'd been hounding her for months, doggedly trying to get her to accept him. Even the significance of her baptism meant nothing to him.

But his photo of her dressing in the window had

been a turning point. It signaled that Trent was becoming far more invasive and brazen. His note was angry and almost taunting. Even the police had agreed.

Hannah and her parents had been sure that Trent's stalking of her was only going to get worse.

However, after the police had informed them that since there were no fingerprints on the note, envelope, or photos, and that it had simply arrived at the restaurant, there was nothing they could do. Hannah was still at Trent's mercy.

When Hannah started shaking so much at the thought of being photographed by Trent again, her father allowed her to quit her job and stay at home.

When another photo of Hannah was mailed to their house, the one of her reading out on her back patio, Hannah stopped even venturing outside. She refused to go to church. She started withdrawing from her work friends. Then she began to avoid Kirsten and her other Amish girlfriends.

But more photos still arrived with alarming regularity.

Then her parents announced that they were going to move to Kentucky, and not to just one of the more populated Amish communities, either.

Instead, they were going to live in Hart County. It was in the middle of the state, in the cavern region. A place not exactly known to be farm friendly.

And it was known to be fairly off the grid, even for the English.

Ben and Jenny hadn't been happy about the move and had been vocal about it. Hannah could see their point. They'd both had lots of friends and part-time jobs. They'd had lives they enjoyed and a house that was both comfortable and their family's legacy. In addition, Berlin was busy and bustling. There were a lot of Amish and a lot of things to do.

Where they were now living in the outskirts of Munfordville? Not so much.

Because of all that, Ben and Jenny had been cross and rude. And because they couldn't take their frustrations out on their parents, they took out their grievances on Hannah.

Which was why she desperately needed a break.

Stepping to the side, Mamm plucked Hannah's black cardigan sweater from the hook. "Enough talk! Put on your sweater and go on a walk."

"I don't know if I can."

"You can if you want to try. Just go, dear. It doesn't have to be for long. Maybe just for thirty minutes."

Thirty minutes. Thirty minutes of freedom. Thirty minutes of putting herself at risk.

If she could do that, she would be proud of herself.

She needed to do that.

Swallowing hard, she nodded. "All right, Muddah. I will give it a try."

Her mother gave a little clap. "*Gut*! Good for you." Then, to Hannah's bemusement, she thrust Hannah's sweater into her arms. And before she could slip one of her arms through a sleeve, Mamm opened the door and kind of shuttled Hannah outside.

"Off you go, now. Enjoy the walk and the fresh air."

Just as Hannah was about to thank her for the push, her mother closed the door.

Staring at the thick panel of oak, she felt a burst of panic bubble up inside her. Before she quite knew what she was doing, she'd reached for the handle.

Then she realized that she was once again going to let her paranoia take hold of her.

"No one is outside this house watching you," she told herself sternly. "No one cares who you are or what you do. You are simply another girl living her life, here in the middle of Kentucky. That's all."

At another time in her life, she might have thought that she was being a little hard on herself. But today, the harsh language seemed to be what she needed.

It was time to stop living in the past and begin thinking about her future. A future without fear. A future where she could be herself once again.

And if she did that, she could also have a future where she wasn't spending most of her time with two siblings who wouldn't want her there in the first place.

Feeling a bit like a small duckling being encouraged to fly, Hannah slipped on her sweater and stepped out from the shade of the porch into the sun.

She had no choice. It was either start walking or return to where she had been. And that place had been so dark and terrifying, she would be a fool to even contemplate doing that.

Feeling like she was on the cusp of something vitally important, she took a deep breath. When she did, she realized the faint scent of freshly cut grass was in the air. Noticed a bright red cardinal off in the distance. It alighted on a branch for a split second before flying off again.

It was time to do a bit of flying of her own. Past time. She started walking.

Chapter 2

July 9

Someone was coming. After reeling in his line, Isaac Troyer set his pole on the bank next to Spot, his Australian shepherd, and turned in the direction of the noise.

He wasn't worried about encountering a stranger as much as curious to know who would walk through the woods while managing to disturb every tree branch, twig, and bird in their midst. A silent tracker, this person was not.

Beside him, Spot, named for the spot of black fur ringing his eye, pricked his ears and tilted his head to one side as he, too, listened and watched for their guest to appear.

When they heard a muffled *umph,* followed by the crack of a branch, Isaac began to grow amused. Their visitor didn't seem to be faring so well.

He wasn't surprised. That path was rarely used and notoriously overrun with hollyhocks, poison oak, and ivy. For some reason, wild rosebushes also ran rampant there. Though walking on the old path made for a pretty journey, it also was a somewhat dangerous one, too. Those bushes had a lot of thorns. Most everyone he knew chose to walk on the road instead.

He was just wondering if, perhaps, he should brave the thorns and the possibility of rashes to offer his help—when a woman popped out.

The new girl. Hannah Hilty.

Obviously thinking she was completely alone, she stepped out of the shade of the bushes and lifted her face into the sun. She mumbled to herself as she pulled a black sweater off her light-blue short-sleeved dress. Then she turned her right arm this way and that, frowning at what looked like a sizable scrape on it.

He'd been introduced to her at church the first weekend her family had come. His first impression of her had been that she was a pretty thing, with dark-brown hair and hazel-colored eyes. She was fairly tall and willowy, too, and had been blessed with creamy-looking pale skin. But for all of that, she'd looked incredibly wary.

Thinking she was simply shy, he'd tried to be friendly, everyone in his family had. But instead of looking happy to meet him or his siblings, she'd merely stared at him the way a doe might stare at an oncoming car—with a bit of weariness and a great dose of fear.

He left her alone after that.

Every once in a while he'd see her. At church, or at the market with her mother. She always acted kind of odd. She was mostly silent, sometimes hardly even talking to her parents or siblings. Often, when he'd see her family in town shopping, she usually wasn't with them. When she was, he'd see her following her parents. With them, yet separate. Silently watching her surroundings like she feared she was about to step off a cliff.

So, by his estimation, she was a strange girl. Weird.

And her actions just now? They seemed even odder. Feeling kind of sorry for her, he got to his feet. "Hey!" he called out.

Obviously startled, Hannah turned to him with a jerk, then froze.

Her unusual hazel eyes appeared dilated. She looked scared to death. Rethinking the step forward he'd been about to do, he stayed where he was. Maybe she wasn't right in the mind? Maybe she was lost and needed help.

Feeling a little worried about her, he held up a hand. "Hey, Hannah. Are you okay?"

But instead of answering him, or even smiling back like a normal person would, she simply stared.

He tried again. "I'm Isaac Troyer." When no look of recognition flickered in her eyes, he added, "I'm your neighbor. We met at church, soon after you moved in. Remember?"

She clenched her fists but otherwise seemed to be trying hard to regain some self-control. After another second, color bloomed in her cheeks. "I'm Hannah Hilty."

"Yeah. I know." Obviously, he'd known it. Hadn't she heard him say her name? He smiled at her, hoping she'd see the humor in their conversation. It was awfully intense for two neighbors having to reacquaint themselves.

By his reckoning, anyway.

She still didn't smile back. Actually, she didn't do much of anything at all, besides gaze kind of blankly at him.

Belatedly, he started wondering if something

had happened to her on her walk. "Hey, are you okay? Are you hurt or something?"

Her hand clenched into a fist. "Why do you ask?"

Everything he wanted to say sounded mean and rude. "You just, uh, seem out of breath." And she was white as a sheet, looked like she'd just seen a monster, and could hardly speak.

Giving her an out, he said, "Are you lost?"

"*Nee.*"

He was starting to lose patience with her. All he'd wanted to do was sit on the bank with Spot and fish for an hour or two, not enter into some strange conversation with his neighbor girl.

"Okay, then. Well, I was just fishing, so I'm going to go back and do that."

Just before he turned away, she took a deep breath. Then she spoke. "I'm sorry. I know I'm not making any sense."

"You're making sense." *Kind of.* "But that said, you don't got anything to be sorry for. It's obvious you, too, were looking for a couple of minutes to be by yourself."

"No, that ain't it." After taking another deep breath, she said, "Seeing you took me by surprise. That's all."

Isaac wasn't enough of a jerk to not be aware that seeing a strange man, when you thought you were alone, might be scary to a timid girl like her.

"You took me by surprise, too. I never see anyone out here."

Some of the muscles in her face and neck relaxed. After another second, she seemed to come to a decision and stepped closer to him. "Is that your dog?"

"*Jah*. His name is Spot, on account of the circle around his eye."

"He looks to be a real fine *hund*." She smiled.

And what a smile it was. Sweet, lighting up her eyes. Feeling a bit taken by surprise, too, he said, "He's an Australian shepherd and real nice. Would you like to meet him?"

"Sure." She smiled again, this time displaying pretty white teeth.

"Spot, come here, boy."

With a stretch and a groan, Spot stood up, stretched again, then sauntered over. When he got to Isaac's side, he paused. Isaac ran a hand along his back, then clicked his tongue, a sign for Spot to simply be a dog.

Spot walked right over and rubbed his nose along one of Hannah's hands.

She giggled softly. "Hello, Spot. Aren't you a handsome *hund*?" After she let Spot sniff her hand, she ran it along his soft fur. Spot, as could be expected, closed his eyes and enjoyed the attention.

"Look at that," Hannah said. "He likes to be petted."

"He's friendly."

"Do you go fishing here much?" she asked hesitantly.

"Not as much as I'd like to. I'm pretty busy. Usually, I'm helping my father on the farm or working in my uncle's woodworking shop." Because she seemed interested, he admitted, "I don't get to sit around and just enjoy the day all that much."

"And here I came and ruined your peace and quiet."

"I didn't say that. You're fine."

She didn't look as if she believed him. Actually, she looked even more agitated. Taking a step backward, she said, "I should probably let you get back to your fishing, then."

"I don't care about that. I'd rather talk to you."

Her eyes widened. "Oh?"

"*Jah.* I mean, we're neighbors and all." When she still looked doubtful, he said, "Besides, every-one is curious about you."

"I don't know why. I'm just an Amish girl."

He thought she was anything but that. "Come on," he chided. "You know what I'm talking about."

Looking even more unsure, she shook her head.

"First off, I've hardly even seen you around town, only on Sundays when we have church. And even then you never stray from your parents' side. That's kind of odd."

"I'm still getting used to being here in Kentucky," she said quickly.

"What is there to get used to?" he joked. "We're just a small community in the middle of cave country."

To his surprise, she stepped back. "I guess getting used to my new home is taking me a while. But that doesn't mean anything."

Aware that he'd hurt her feelings, he realized that he should have really watched his tone. "Sorry. I didn't mean to offend you. I was just saying that the way you've been acting has everyone curious. That's why people are calling you 'The Recluse.'"

" 'The Recluse'?"

"Well, *jah*. I mean you truly are an Amish woman of mystery," he said, hoping she'd tease him right back like his older sister would have done.

She did not.

Actually, she looked like she was about to cry, and it was his doing.

When was he ever going to learn to read people better? Actually, he should knock some sense into himself. He'd been a real jerk. "Sorry. I didn't intend to sound so callous."

"Well, you certainly did."

"Ah, you are right. It was a bad joke."

"I better go."

Staring at her more closely, he noticed that

those pretty hazel eyes of hers looked kind of shimmery, like a whole mess of tears was about to fall. Now he felt worse than bad. "Hey, are you going to be okay getting home? I could walk you back, if you'd like."

"*Danke, nee.*"

Reaching out, he grasped Spot by his collar. "I don't mind at all. It will give us a chance to—"

She cut him off. "I do not want or need your help." She was staring at him like he was scary. Like he was the type of guy who would do her harm.

That bothered him.

"Look, I already apologized. You don't need to look at me like I'm going to attack you or something. I'm just trying to be a good neighbor."

She flinched before visibly collecting herself. "I understand. But like I said, I don't want your help. I will be fine."

When he noticed that Spot was also sensing her distress, he tried again even though he knew he should just let her go. "I was done fishing anyway. All I have to do is grab my pole. Then Spot and I could walk with you."

"What else do I have to say for you to listen to me?" she fairly cried out. "Isaac, I do not want you to walk me anywhere." She turned and darted away, sliding back into the brush. No doubt about to get covered in more scratches and poison ivy.

Well, she'd finally said his name, and it certainly did sound sweet on her lips.

Too bad she was now certain to avoid him for the rest of her life.

He really hoped his mother was never going to hear about how awful he'd just been. She'd be so disappointed.

He was disappointed in himself, and was usually a lot more patient with people. He liked that about himself, too. And this girl? Well, she needed someone, too. But she seemed even afraid of her shadow.

Chapter 3

July 9

The moment she left Isaac's sight, Hannah decided one thing for sure and for certain. She did not want to converse with Isaac Troyer ever again.

He was rude. He joked about things he shouldn't, too.

After all, what kind of man was he? Who went about calling people they didn't know mean names, then went ahead and shared them?

A rude man. That was who!

She was fuming so much as she walked up her short driveway, she almost didn't notice the trio of clay pots filled with blooming daisies resting to the left of their mail box. She might have missed them completely if their sweet perfume hadn't been clinging to the air, practically pulling her toward them.

As their scent engulfed her and clouded her senses, she started to feel sick.

Trent used to give her daisies all the time. He'd buy her dozens of them from the local florists or greenhouses, wrap them in tissue paper or tie a ribbon around them, and give them to her with a smile.

Every single time he did that, he would say something about how daisies were so like her. So fresh. So innocent. So perfect.

The first time he'd said such things, she'd been foolish enough to be taken in by the meaningless words. She'd thought the words were sweet and original. She'd thought the daisies were special and that his efforts meant that she was more than she'd ever imagined she was.

But then, his gifts had begun to feel like pressure. He'd wanted more flattery, more appreciation, more of all of her.

She hadn't ever been able to give him enough.

Now the daisies only symbolized just how mistaken she'd been to let her vanity get the best of her. How foolish she'd been to ever trust an Englisher in the first place.

Seeing the three pots overfilling with blooms

felt like a terrible betrayal. After all, everyone in the family knew she could hardly stand to look at those flowers. Who would have purchased them and set them out for her to see the moment she got back from her walk?

She was tempted to carry each pot across the road. There was a dark thicket of woods there. If she used all her strength, she could probably toss each one far enough into the woods that they'd be hidden from view. It was likely no one would see them for weeks, maybe even months.

Only a need to discover who had brought the daisies to their property kept them in place. But it didn't curb her anger.

"What are you glaring at?" Ben asked.

Startled, she turned to see that he was lounging on one of the brightly painted lounge chairs on the front porch.

"Did you bring those flowers home?"

"What flowers?"

"Those," she said, pointing to the daisies like they were angry dogs poised to attack.

He stood up and stared in the direction she was pointing. "What flowers? Oh. Those daisies?"

His obvious confusion served to take some of the anger out of her sails. "Yes. Do you know where they came from?"

"*Nee.*" He continued to stare at her as if she had lost her mind, which was a pretty constant look these days.

"Are you sure?"

"I'm positive. I don't go looking at pots of daisies, Hannah," he said, his voice thick with irritation. "I didn't even notice them. But if I had, I probably would have moved them. I have no desire to go around doing things to make you upset."

Feeling embarrassed, she struggled to regain her composure. "I know you don't. I'm sorry for practically attacking you like that. I was already upset and, when I saw those flowers, something inside of me snapped."

"Why were you so upset? Where did you go, anyway?"

Though she wanted nothing more than to go straight inside and retreat into the comfort and security of her room, Hannah knew she should at least try to converse with him.

Walking up the steps, she sat down on a chair next to him. Now that they were closer, she noticed that his light-blue shirt was untucked, he was barefoot, and his straw hat was pushed back so she could see the majority of his wheat-colored bangs.

He was a handsome boy. He'd always been. Already the girls were giving him second and third looks, which he pretended he didn't notice.

He also was looking fairly irritated, which was slowly becoming the norm with him. No matter what happened to him in Munfordville, he seemed determined to find fault with it. She knew he firmly placed the blame of his unhappiness on her shoulders. Though she hadn't asked for anything that had happened to her, she figured it was only natural to resent the cause of his unhappiness.

Because he seemed a little more content than he had been in weeks, she answered him patiently. "I went for a walk. Why?"

He threw her an impatient glare. "You never leave the *haus*, Hannah."

"I do."

"*Jah*. For church." He rolled his eyes. "Which means you leave once every two weeks. That pretty much counts as never."

"Not really. And for the record, I leave the house more than that. You know I do the shopping with Mamm," she said with a small lift of her chin, even though she knew better than to get into a war of words with her brother. He delighted in verbal battles.

"Shopping at the market with Mamm don't count," he said sagely.

She figured it kind of didn't, either. Whenever she ventured out with their mother, Hannah hardly left her mother's side, and she never spoke to another person if she didn't absolutely have to.

However, she had left the house today, all by herself. And even though it hadn't gone all that well—that boy, that Isaac, was awfully full of himself—she still had done it. And because of that, she felt a little more self-confident than she had been in months.

"Never mind what I've been doing." Looking Ben in the eye, she said, "Why are you sitting out here by yourself? That isn't like you."

And just like that, his demeanor changed from surly teen to excited boy. "I'm waiting for someone."

"Really? Who?"

"A boy about my age. He's coming over to get me and show me around." Looking even more confident, he said, "He's a friend."

For the first time since she'd gotten home, she smiled. She really was happy for Ben. Before they'd left Berlin, he'd had a ton of friends and was always busy. He'd been having a particularly hard time adjusting to living in a much smaller town and not knowing anyone. "Who is this friend you made?"

"Sam Troyer. He lives on the farm next to us."

He had to be Isaac's brother. A flicker of unease settled inside of her, though she had no idea why. She had nothing to fear from teenagers.

Knowing that and acting like a reasonable woman were two different things, however. "Be careful."

"We're just going to walk around, Hannah. There ain't anything to be careful about."

"Still . . . things happen."

34

"Fine. I'll do my best to make sure no one takes my picture or anything," he said sarcastically.

His comment hurt. She hated that he felt comfortable making comments about the actions that had changed her life.

But then she had to remember that those events had changed his life, too. He'd been uprooted from everything he'd ever known in practically the blink of an eye.

Therefore, instead of chastising him, she walked right by and at last opened the door and strode inside. Maybe she should talk to her parents about the Troyers. After all, who knew what this Sam was like. She probably should tell them about her conversation with Isaac, too.

"Hannah, is that you?" her father called out from their small living room.

Curious as to why he was already sitting in the living room instead of out working in the yard, she walked over to him. "*Jah*, it's me."

He pulled off his reading glasses and squinted up at her. "Did you have a nice walk?"

"It was all right." Noticing that he was sitting alone and the kitchen sounded quieter than usual, she asked, "Where's Mamm?"

"She'll be back soon. She, ah, had an appointment in town."

Hannah thought he sounded evasive. But maybe that was simply her imagination? "And Jenny?"

"I think Jenny is in her room working on the homework you assigned her," he replied with a smile.

"*Gut*. I've been nagging her something awful about it."

"I heard. She showed me what you assigned. You are a hard taskmaster."

"Not so much." Noticing that the lines around her father's eyes were more pronounced than usual, she said, "Are you feeling okay, Daed?"

He looked down at his sleeve and pulled a stray thread off of one of the seams. "Of course. A man can take an afternoon off if he wants it every now and then. Ain't so?"

Hannah noticed that his weak smile didn't reach his eyes. "Yes. Of course." Right then and there she pushed aside her notion of talking to her father about how rude and brash Isaac was. She didn't know what was on her father's mind, but she had a strong feeling that it was much more important than her paranoia about her neighbors.

"I'm going to my room for a little while. I'll check on Jenny, too," she said.

Her father didn't answer, just slipped back on his glasses and lifted up his newspaper again.

Hannah walked down the hall to the room she shared with her little sister, mentally bracing herself for the abuse that was about to come. Jenny was barely civil on her best days. Today,

36

after working on assignments she hadn't wanted to do in the first place?—Jenny was going to be churlish indeed.

It was moments like this when she longed for her old house and her old room.

Their house in Berlin was easily double the size of their current one. It had been a two-story farmhouse with a full basement, too. It also had a full front porch and a large back patio that her father had made out of brick. But the best part of that old house had been her beautiful bedroom. It had been large, almost as large as her parents'. It also had two large picture windows that faced the front yard and let in tons of sunlight. She and her mother had painted the walls a pale yellow. It had been such a warm and inviting place.

She'd also had a padded white rocking chair, a pretty desk and chair, a queen-sized bed, and her very own window seat. Kirsten often teased Hannah that she had a room fit for a fairytale princess instead of a regular old Amish girl. Hannah figured her best friend had a point, but she'd loved it nonetheless.

After Trent's photo, everything in her sanctuary had felt tainted. Her privacy had been violated and each piece of furniture—especially her dressing table—had seemed to symbolize her loss of innocence.

When they moved, her parents had sold their bedroom set and taken hers. She'd been in such a daze at the time, she'd hardly cared about what they'd done.

Every time she walked into her room and saw Jenny's old stuffed animals and clothes on one side of the room, and spied her own very utilitarian-looking twin bed, Hannah felt as if she'd lost something very dear to her.

Now she not only didn't have a princess room, she had no privacy, either. Everything she'd loved —the checkered window seat, the yellow walls, the large flowered comforter, the white rocking chair—it was all gone.

When she opened the door, Jenny, who was sitting on her bed with a book in her lap, looked up and scowled. "You're back."

Hannah tried to ignore the comment. It was nothing Jenny hadn't said to her a dozen times. Her pretty, slim, petulant sister had always seemed at a loss of what to do with Hannah now that they were living in each other's pockets, and Hannah was acting so different than the way she used to. Jenny also had no patience with Hannah's new irrational fear of the world outside her door.

"I talked to Daed. He said Mamm was on an appointment. What kind? Is she at the doctor? Is she sick or something?"

"*Nee*. She went for a job interview."

Hannah sat down on the opposite twin bed. "Why? What kind of job?"

Jenny shrugged. "I don't know. You know Mamm and Daed," she said in an off-hand manner that she'd recently adopted. "They don't tell us anything."

"I know they like to keep things to themselves, but I'm still pretty surprised."

"I don't know why. They love to keep secrets." While Hannah gaped at her, Jenny continued, waving her hands a bit to emphasize various words and phrases. "First, they moved us here into the middle of Kentucky without any warning. Then, they chose this house without a word of explanation."

"There's nothing wrong with this house," Hannah retorted, though she'd been thinking the same thing just a couple of minutes ago.

"You're right. There isn't . . . if one was used to living in a house this size." Jenny exhaled. "Hannah, it's so small. Really small. Even when I asked why they chose to buy a house that was so different, on a small lot instead of a place like our farm, they told me it weren't none of my business."

"They were kind of right, Jenny."

Jenny stared hard at her. "Were they? I know I don't pay any bills or anything, but I live here, and I'm likely gonna be living here for several more years, too. Far longer than you."

Her sister was voicing things that Hannah had thought from time to time, but had been too preoccupied to dwell upon. Now she wished she'd been more aware of what was going on and how her sister was reacting to it all. "I think you have a point."

"I know I do."

Jenny closed the book on her lap, the book Hannah now realized had absolutely nothing to do with homework. It was a paperback romance novel, and Hannah had no idea how she'd gotten ahold of it. "What is that you are reading?" she blurted.

"Nothing for you to worry about. What is important is that something is going on with our parents and someone needs to find out what that is."

"I can't believe you've noticed all of that and I didn't. I guess I've been pretty oblivious."

Jenny wrinkled her freckled nose. "You're only now realizing that?"

In the last two hours, Hannah had had quite a number of uncomfortable conversations, each one pointing out another flaw in her character. She was getting pretty tired of it.

"Realizing what, Jenny? If you are going to accuse me of something, at least be open and honest."

Jenny uncrossed her legs and shifted so that she was facing Hannah directly. "Do you really want to hear honesty, or are you just going to go all fragile again?"

The question was hard to hear. It was also mean and—Hannah was a bit afraid to admit to herself—true. She had been so scared and traumatized by Trent's flowers and notes and stalking that she'd ignored most of everything else that had been happening around her.

She also realized, with a bit of dismay, she had been allowing her little brother, sister, and parents to coddle her. Maybe she'd even expected all of them to make amends for her, too.

And now her little sister had nothing of meaning to say to her anymore.

That had to stop. "I want to hear what's on your mind, sister."

"All right, then. We had to move because of *you*. Instead of going to the police right away or trying to get that Trent to stop, our parents practically ran away."

"No, they did talk to the sheriff."

"But did they listen when the sheriff told them that it was going to take time to get enough evidence to arrest him? Of course they didn't! They just sold everything and moved. Daed quit his job. We moved out of our pretty house on the hill to this place. Now Daed is pretending to garden and he doesn't even like to garden. And Mamm is going to be working. Ben and I had to leave all of our friends. We even had to quit school and agree to get homeschooled by you because mother said the Amish school is too far away."

"All of what happened isn't my fault. I didn't ask Mamm and Daed to move."

"It might as well be," Jenny said, tears forming in her eyes. "Not that you care."

"Of course I care about what is happening. I didn't want any of this to happen. You don't understand how Trent was."

"I understand that he's back in Ohio. He's probably moved on to another girl to bother while you won't hardly leave the house."

"I left today."

"So what? No doubt you came home acting like it was the worst experience of your life. So now, our parents are going to circle around you again. And Ben and I are going to have to be careful again. Watch every word we say so we don't accidentally hurt your feelings. Or stir up bad memories . . . that you don't seem to want to forget." She rolled her eyes.

Stunned by her sister's caustic words, Hannah stood up. "I'm sorry you're so upset and angry with me. I'm sorry you think I either don't care about what's happened to you, or that I'm in some way responsible for all of your problems. I feel bad for you, I do. But I'm also happy for you, too."

"Happy?"

"Oh, yes. Because if you had any idea about how it feels to go through what I've been going through, you'd understand. And if you understood, then we'd both know how awful it's been for me. And I would never wish that on anyone. Most especially you."

"There is one thing you have failed to understand, sister," Jenny whispered.

"And what is that?"

"That it's over. Trent's fixation is all over, but you refuse to let it go. And because you won't let it go, all of us have to keep suffering, too. Every. Single. Day."

Jenny rolled on her side and picked up her book.

Hannah had no idea if she was reading or not. All she could think about was that her sister was probably right.

She needed to stop worrying about being hurt again or that Trent would someday find her. No one would ever be that determined.

With that in mind, she decided not to ask Jenny about whether or not she had set those pots of daisies in their yard. Jenny wouldn't have done such a thing.

It was probably a silly coincidence. A silly coincidence that no one but her would ever notice anyway.

Chapter 4

July 9

"I caught you two fish, Mamm," Isaac hollered when he entered the kitchen. "Trout. Good size, too."

His mother poked her head out of their large walk-in pantry. "And what fine fish they are. Why, they look good enough to eat."

He smiled at the same joke she'd been spouting, pretty much, forever. "They will be." Holding them over the basin, he said, "Where do you want them? Here, in the sink?"

"You may put them on a plate . . . after you go back outside and clean them."

He groaned. "You know I hate cleaning fish."

"You get that aversion naturally, son. I dislike it as well. But it is your job, not mine. Ain't so?"

Technically, yes. But if he could get his brother to do it, he would. "Where's Sam?" he asked hopefully. His brother took after his father. A natural hunter and fisherman, Sam could fillet a fish in record time. He never complained about it, either.

"You're out of luck, I'm afraid. He's out with Ben Hilty."

It took Isaac a minute to place the name. Then it clicked. "Ben is our new neighbor, yes?"

"*Jah.*" Walking out of the pantry holding two jars of canned peaches, she said, "Sam has been after me for days to give him some time to go play with our new neighbor. Since he came home on Friday with good grades, I decided to let him have most of today off from his chores."

"You mean hang out, Mamm. Thirteen-year-old boys don't play."

She rolled her eyes, not looking fazed in the slightest by the correction. "I'm mother to four *kinner.* You call it what you want. I'll call it playing."

"Fair enough." Knowing he couldn't procrastinate much longer, he said, "I'll be back in when these fish are filleted."

"*Danke*, Isaac."

After grabbing a sharp knife, a bucket, and a plastic cutting board, he wandered out to the barn and got busy doing the dreaded task.

Kneeling on the ground, he neatly chopped off one head, tossed it in the bucket, then began running the knife along the side of the fish like his father had taught him so long ago. When he was pleased with his efforts for the first, he turned on the hose and rinsed off the knife and work area.

He was about to start on the second when he saw Samuel with their new neighbor coming up the hill.

When Sam saw what Isaac was doing, he grinned. "Mamm didn't let you get out of it?"

"*Nee*. I tried to see if you could do it, though." Eyeing the sandy-haired teen, Isaac added, "She said you had plans with our new neighbor."

"*Jah*. This here is Ben Hilty. Ben, this is my big brother, Isaac."

Ben held up a hand. "Hiya."

"Hi to you, too," Isaac said as he began running his knife down his second catch. "I hope you are settling into Munfordville. You've been here a couple of months now. Ain't so?"

"Three," the teen said as he watched Isaac make a second slice.

If Isaac wasn't mistaken, Ben was a little green around the gills. He set down his knife and stared at their new neighbor. "You all right?"

Sam looked at Ben and laughed. "What's wrong with ya? You look like you're about to throw up."

Ben pressed his hands to his stomach. "The insides of fish look pretty gross."

"They do take some getting used to," Isaac said. "Unless you're Sam."

Ben looked at Sam curiously. "Why is that? Do you like cutting up fish?"

Sam chuckled again. "It ain't my favorite thing to do, but it's all right. It really don't bother me that much. Course, that's probably because I've been doing it for so long."

"Don't let him fool you," Isaac said. "I've been cleaning fish most of my life and I still try to get out of it. Our older sister, Mary, doesn't even like to cook, let alone fillet fish."

"Luckily, her husband, James, likes to both fish and clean them," Sam said.

"This is true. We can only hope that little Freeman will take after Sam instead of me."

"So there are four of you?" Ben asked.

"Yep. Mary, then me, Sam, and finally seven-year-old Freeman," Isaac said. "Mary is married and lives over in Horse Cave. I take after my grandfather and do mostly woodworking. Sam here is our father's son through and through. Sam excels at all things outdoorsy. And then there's Freeman, who is the most thoughtful and subdued of us all. We're a varied lot."

Sam stared at him curiously. "What about you, Ben? Do you like fishing?"

"I don't know," Ben said. "I've never been fishing."

Sam stared at him in surprise. "Never?"

"Never. Fishing isn't something my family likes to do." Looking a bit contemplative, he added, "At least, we didn't back in Ohio."

"Welcome to Kentucky," Isaac said. "Around here, pretty much every boy grows up hunting and fishing. And learning how to clean and prepare whatever it is we get."

Sam nodded. "I've been hunting since I was

Freeman's age. I got my first rabbit when I was seven," he said proudly. "Do you hunt?"

This time Ben looked embarrassed. "*Nee*. I ain't ever been hunting, either."

"Next time my *daed* takes me, I'll ask him if you can come along," Sam said easily. "If you want to go, that is."

Excitement lit their neighbor's eyes. "*Danke*. I would like that."

Now that his fish were nicely filleted, Isaac tied up the contents of the bucket, tossed them in the trash, and rinsed off his hands, knife, and cutting board again. "Sam, it looks like you're going to have a great time teaching Ben all about living out in the country."

"I guess so." Looking curiously at his new friend, Sam said, "If you didn't go hunting and fishing, what did you do out in Ohio?"

"I helped out with our farm."

"You had a farm?" Sam asked.

"*Jah*. We had a big farm and a big house, too. We grew corn and harvested it every fall. Of course, I also went to school. Last year, I got my first real job. I helped out at a motel down the street."

Sam's eyes widened. "You worked in a real motel?"

"*Jah*." Sounding much more confident, Ben continued. "We lived in Berlin, and it's a popular tourist spot. It was a busy place, especially in the spring and fall. There was always something to do."

Isaac felt sorry for the boy. He looked and sounded a little lost. "I bet our country way of life is taking some getting used to."

"Yeah, it is. My sister and I still can't believe we're here."

"It ain't so bad here," Sam blurted.

"I know," Ben said quickly. "I'm not trying to sound mean, it's just real different. Everything about our life here is different." He shrugged. "I'm still getting used to it."

Still looking a bit defensive, Sam said, "If you were so happy there, why did you move?"

"Samuel, don't be rude," Isaac interjected. "That ain't none of our business."

"I'm just asking." Looking at Ben, Sam muttered, "But just because I asked, it don't mean you have to answer me."

Ben clenched his hands, then slowly relaxed them. At last, he blurted, "We had to because of my sister."

"Really? What happened with Jenny?" Sam asked.

"Nothing happened to her. We had to move because of my *older* sister." His voice turned flat. "Hannah."

"Huh," Isaac said. He'd given up even pretending he wasn't interested in Ben's story.

Sam looked puzzled. "Hannah? Oh, yeah. She's

the one who never leaves your *haus*. Is there something wrong with her?" asked Sam.

Isaac glared at his little brother.

"What? It's true. Plus, you noticed it first. Remember? You even called her The Recluse." Sam snickered.

Which shamed Isaac something awful.

When Ben turned to him, a combination of hurt and anger in his eyes, Isaac knew that condemnation was no less than he deserved. He'd been cruel, and worse, he'd passed on his bad behavior to his little brother. "Ben, I am sorry. I did call Hannah that, but it was wrong of me to say such things. I don't even know why I did. I promise that I won't call Hannah that again."

"I hope not," Ben retorted. "Just because she's been through a terrible time, it don't mean that you can make fun of her."

"I'm sorry she's been through a hard time," Isaac said. "And you are right. Like I said, what I did was wrong. I'm ashamed of myself."

"What happened to her that was so terrible?" Sam asked. "Did she get real sick or something?"

"*Nee*. Nothing like that." Ben hesitated, then blurted, "Hannah had a stalker back in Berlin."

Sam's brows pulled together. "What's that?"

"A person who becomes attached to someone and follows them around."

"Someone got attached to your sister?"

"*Jah.* An Englisher man followed her around and took pictures of her. He wrote her notes, too. He was creepy." His voice hardened. "That means she's got a real good reason for not liking to go outside."

Sam stared. "Why was he taking pictures of her? Was he a tourist or something and wanted photos of the Amish to show his friends?"

"*Nee,* it wasn't like that. He wasn't taking pictures of the Amish. He was taking pictures of her. He only wanted photos of Hannah. She didn't know when he was doing it, either."

Not wanting to simply stare at Ben, Isaac started rolling up the garden hose. But he was still listening to every word . . . and feeling worse by the second about how he'd acted toward Hannah.

"My parents even had to talk to the police," Ben continued. "But because there were no finger-prints on anything, they couldn't prove that this man was doing everything. That's when Hannah got even more upset and scared. She got so bad that we had to leave."

"Wow," Sam exclaimed. "I bet you were really mad about that."

"*Jah.* I have been. It weren't Hannah's fault, though," he said quickly. "Hannah had a job and friends. She never did anything to deserve what he did. This man simply picked her out."

"She had a lot of reasons to be scared, didn't she?" Sam mumbled.

"*Jah.* I guess she did." Looking a bit empty, Ben said, "Hannah ain't over it, either. That's why she still acts afraid of her shadow."

While Sam continued to stare at Ben like he'd grown two heads, Isaac felt even worse. That poor girl had gone out on a walk and he'd done nothing but talk to her like she should be happy they were having a conversation. Then, when she hadn't acted that way, he'd acted smug. He owed her an apology.

He owed her brother a better apology, too.

It was obvious that Ben was lost and unhappy; and here, the first time he comes over to their house to be with Sam, they badger him about Hannah. "Listen, I'm sorry we asked so many questions. What happened to her wasn't any of our business. I'm real sorry about your sister, too. I hope she will get to be feeling better soon."

Ben looked caught off guard, then slowly nodded. *"Danke."*

After giving Sam a meaningful look, one that he hopefully took to mean that he needed to be extra friendly, Isaac went back into the kitchen.

His mother was at the stove, a cast-iron skillet on the range and a bowl of cornmeal, and another of eggs and milk, in front of her. "At last! I got out everything to fry the fish, then you didn't come in."

"Sorry. It took me a while."

"I saw you talking to Sam and Ben. Our new neighbor seems like a nice boy, don't you think so?"

"Yeah." Isaac debated whether or not to tell his mom about what he heard, but he decided he needed her advice. "Hey, Mamm, I've got a story for you."

She held out her hands for the cutting board full of fish. "You can tell me while I fry up your catch."

After washing his hands, he sat down on one of the barstools surrounding the counter. "I think I made a huge mistake. I managed to offend both Ben and his older sister, Hannah, today."

"You better start at the beginning, Isaac."

So, he did. He told her about fishing and spying Hannah coming out of the woods. He told her how he'd called her The Recluse and had hurt her feelings. Then, how Sam had even shared that with Ben.

His mother winced. "Oh, dear."

"*Jah*, Mamm. But it gets worse." After taking a fortifying breath, he relayed what Ben had told them about what had happened to her back in Berlin.

Her eyes widened. "That poor girl."

"I know, Mamm. She's had a real tough time of it."

As she moved the fish in the hot oil, his mother said, "I'll speak to Sam. I'll make sure he knows to be nicer to her, and to reach out to her brother, too. That family needs some compassion."

"Yeah, they sure do."

Not noticing how lost Isaac sounded, his mother continued. "What's more, that boy needs to be reminded that we never know what other people are going through until we spend time in their shoes. He needs to behave better and not be so judgmental. It's not only the right way to behave—he's a role model as well. Freeman watches everything he does, you know."

Though she mentioned Sam's name, Isaac knew she was speaking to him. He was Sam's role model.

She was upset with him, and he deserved her disappointment, too.

Now Isaac felt even worse. What had possessed him to act so childishly in the first place? He knew better. After being hospitalized with meningitis when he was thirteen, Isaac had vowed to treat others with kindness. He'd learned that one never knew what other people were going through or recovering from.

How had he forgotten that? "Mamm, kids Sam's age say thoughtless things all the time. But I'm twenty-two. I know better."

"You do. I'm certain you were taught to behave better." Flipping the fish in the hot oil, she shrugged. "That said, you are also human, son. Everyone says things they shouldn't from time to time."

"I need to make amends."

Her expression softened. "What do you think you should do?"

"Go over and ask to speak to her. Then I'll apologize."

"That's a good start."

"I'll talk to Sam, too. He needs to know that I was wrong and that I'm anxious to make things right."

"If you talk to him, I'm sure he'll do whatever you suggest. He likes to do whatever his brother wants him to do."

He knew that. His little brother had always wanted to tag after him, just like he'd often tagged after Mary, their twenty-seven-year-old sister. Now she was married to James and had two babies of her own.

He'd always been close to Mary, maybe because they'd grown up feeling responsible for their two baby brothers. Oh, there had been times when both he and Mary had thoroughly resented having to look after the younger siblings, but that didn't last long. Probably because their father said over and over that they should both value their younger siblings' feelings and understand that such devotion carried a huge responsibility.

They were both role models.

When he was younger, that hadn't been an easy burden to bear. He hadn't wanted to be anyone's role model. Eventually, however, he'd enjoyed

Sam's attention. And as for Freeman? Well, their little towheaded sibling was quiet and studious. So different from them all, but also mighty easy to be around.

Only today did he finally understand what his father had meant about bearing responsibility for one's actions.

"I'll go over there tomorrow, Mamm."

"Tomorrow is for the Lord, Isaac," she murmured as she removed the last fillet from the pan.

"All right. Monday evening, then. I don't know what I'll say, but I'll pray on it tonight. Maybe the Lord will take pity on me and give me some guidance."

"Oh, I imagine He might." Smiling, she pushed a dish with some fried fish strips on it toward him. "After all, you did a mighty good job fishing for us today."

Taking a bite, he shook his head at his mother's silly statement. But he couldn't deny that the fried fish did taste pretty good.

Chapter 5

"I don't understand why we have to write so many letters, Hannah," Jenny complained around nine on Monday morning.

The three of them, Jenny, Ben, and Hannah, were sitting at the kitchen table, working on assignments. Well, Jenny and Ben were. Kind of.

Hannah was attempting to teach them how to work on their spelling skills. As usual, it wasn't going so well.

"Because it's a good way for you to practice your English," Hannah said for what had to be the tenth time that morning. "All Amish men and women need to know how to write properly in English. You should remember that from school in Berlin."

"We never had to write this much." Glaring at her paper, Jenny said, "And I don't care what anyone says, looking up a word in the dictionary to figure out how to spell it makes no sense."

Hannah grinned. "I don't think you're the first person to think that. But that's the best way to check your spelling."

"If we had cell phones, we could use them to help us," Ben said.

Hannah would be lying if she hadn't thought the same thing many times. "Unfortunately, I don't have one. And you don't, either. That is why we are using dictionaries."

"Not yet. But the minute I start my *rumspringa*, I'm gonna get one," Jenny declared. "It's going to be great."

"Good luck with that," Hannah said. "Mamm and Daed wouldn't let me get a cell phone during my *rumspringa* and all of my girlfriends got them."

"Mamm will let me get one. I know she will," Jenny said with a confident look.

"Oh, brother," Ben said. "Here she goes again. Hannah, can I stop now? I wrote my two letters like you wanted me to."

"*Jah*, sure," she said. After Ben walked down the hall to his room, Hannah stared at Jenny. "Why are you so positive that Mamm will get you a phone?"

"Because she feels guilty about moving us all here. She knows I've been miserable."

And here they went again. It seemed hardly a day could go by without one of her siblings bringing up the move and their irritation about it. Though it set her teeth on edge, Hannah decided to tackle the subject head-on. "It wasn't Mamm's fault. Or Daed's, either," she said quietly. "It was mine, and you know it, too. You don't need to pretend otherwise."

Looking a little shamefaced, Jenny sighed. "I'm

not trying to do that. And no matter what you think, I'm trying to learn to like it here. It would be easier if everything wasn't so different."

"I know it's different. I'm finding it that way, too," she confided as the door opened and her parents came inside. "Hiya," she called out. "Did you get your errands done?"

"More or less," Mamm said cryptically.

After eyeing the two of them sitting at the kitchen table, their parents looked at each other and seemed to come to a decision.

"Girls, we need to talk to you about something," Daed began. Looking around the room, he frowned. "Where is Ben?"

"In his room," Jenny replied.

"Go get him," Daed ordered as he sat down next to Hannah. "Tell him to come and join us."

While Jenny walked down the hall to get Ben, her mother sat down with a weary sigh. She looked tired.

"Mamm, do you want some coffee or water or something?"

"Not right now," she murmured as she rubbed her temples. "I had quite a bit of coffee at the— Earlier today."

Hannah noticed that her father was looking tired, too. Maybe even worse. When Jenny and Ben joined them, they looked wary, as if they were mentally preparing themselves for more bad news.

Ben didn't even try to hurry their parents to start speaking. Instead, he placed his hands flat on the seat of his chair, a habit he'd done since he was four or five years old.

After sharing another look with their mother, their father spoke. "We have something to tell you. Something that we probably should have shared weeks ago," he said. "You see . . . there's, well . . . there's another reason we moved here to Munfordville and it has nothing to do with Hannah being stalked by that Englisher."

"What is it?" Jenny asked.

"I have cancer."

Hannah felt like the wind had just been knocked out of her. She felt dizzy, too. As she tried to process what she heard, Ben gasped and Jenny started crying.

After a few seconds passed, Hannah said, "Daed, you said you should have told us weeks ago. When did you find out?"

"Shortly after you brought home those photos that Trent took of you. I'd been coughing a lot, you see, and no medicine seemed to help."

Coughing? "What kind of cancer is it?"

"Lung cancer." Scratching his head, he said, "The doctor said that some folks get it who don't smoke."

"We can't pretend to understand," their mother murmured as she rubbed their father's back. "Only come to terms with it."

Hannah agreed with their mother's pronouncement, but it was definitely hard to do. Especially when she was still feeling so shocked.

"I don't understand why we had to move if you have cancer, Daed," Jenny blurted. "We lived close to the hospital back in Berlin. I heard it's a real *gut* one, too."

He patted her hand. "It is a good one, but I don't plan on visiting the hospital anytime soon."

"Why not?" Hannah asked. "Don't you have to go there for chemotherapy treatments?" She remembered Kennedy, her manager at the country store, talking about her mother's chemo treatments. It seemed they were always going back and forth to the hospital.

"People do have to go there for chemotherapy," their father agreed. "But I'm not going to be having those treatments."

Ben wrinkled his nose. "But I thought everyone did that."

"*Jah*. After all, ain't that how people get better?" Jenny asked. Brightening, she said, "Hey, remember Anne Marie's mother? She had breast cancer, got chemo and surgery and now she's okay."

"Or can this kind of cancer not be treated like that?" Hannah asked.

"It can be treated," Mamm said slowly. "But your father has decided not to treat it."

"God had a reason for me to get lung cancer,"

he said with conviction. "I don't want to interfere with His wishes."

At last, what they were saying sunk in. "So you are telling us that Daed has lung cancer and is going to die from it," Hannah whispered.

"If the Lord doesn't heal him, yes," Mamm said.

Ben looked angry. "But that makes no sense."

"It makes perfect sense," their father said, his tone hard. "I'm a God-fearing man and I'm going to follow His word and His will."

Around a sigh, their mother said, "Today, we met with a local doctor and told him our wishes. He's going to give your father some medicine for any pain he might be experiencing." After looking like she was bracing herself, Mamm added, "We also had to give the hospital all my employment information."

Hannah was mystified. "What employment information?"

"I got a job. I'm going to be working in a shipping company near here. They need someone to help take phone orders, and to pack boxes and prepare them to be shipped. It's a real *gut* job."

"You had all of this in mind when we moved here, didn't you?" Jenny curved her hands around the arms of her chair, as if she needed its support.

"We did. We got a good price on the house and land. Here, we bought a smaller house. That money allows your father to stay home and rest. I had been talking to folks about jobs, too." She smiled weakly. "So today is kind of a big day. I have a job and your father has a plan."

"And you decided to tell us a big secret," Ben said slowly. He blinked. Blinked again. "I canna believe you are so sick, Daed," he said, his voice raspy and strained. "This is terrible news."

"I know my news has been hard to hear, but we are going to be all right."

"Not really," Ben said. "You ain't going to get better. Not at all."

Jenny was crying openly now. "Why is everything happening to us?" she asked. "It's not fair."

"The Lord didn't promise us fairness, child," Daed said, his voice sounding as strained as the rest of them undoubtedly felt. "He only promised that we would get to live our lives in the way He planned for us."

"Well, I sure wish He would have warned me that my life was going to be like this," Jenny said as she got up and ran to her room. "It would have been nice to be prepared."

Leaning back in her chair, Hannah closed her eyes. It didn't happen very often, but at that moment, she was in complete agreement with her sister.

Chapter 6

Monday, July 11

Using her mother's need for a fresh gallon of milk as an excuse, Jenny headed into town. After her parents had calmly shared their real reason for moving them to Kentucky, she'd been in a daze.

No matter how hard she'd tried to think of anything else, even attempting to lose herself in one of her forbidden books, nothing could block out the pain she was feeling.

Or the guilt.

For three months now, she'd concentrated all of her bitterness and confusion and placed it firmly on her older sister's shoulders. Even her heart had told her that her resentment toward Hannah wasn't fair, yet she'd continued to be difficult and mean.

Even when her brain had figured out that Hannah's stalker wasn't going to quit and that they'd needed to do something to help her, Jenny had continued to blame her sister.

Now she was being forced to not only realize that she'd been so very unfair, but there was a whole other matter that was so much more important.

Her father had cancer. Her father was going to die.

Her throat tightened again as she imagined a life without him. Imagined him suffering. Thought about their mother having to continue on her own without Daed by her side.

It wasn't just unfair, it was heartbreaking.

Two hours after her parents had told them their news, she'd been unable to stand her own company. Venturing out into the kitchen, she'd found her mother sitting alone at the table, staring blankly at one of her cookbooks. When she'd mentioned that she was trying to find the strength to go get a gallon of milk, Jenny had jumped at the chance to be of help.

Her mother had accepted gratefully.

One of the benefits to their new house was that it was on a small lot in town, not nestled in the middle of several acres of farmland like their previous one. Because of that, it was fairly easy for all of them to walk to wherever they needed to go.

One of the first places she'd started visiting on her own was A&L Grocery. It was just a small, quaint store. It had a good deli and bakery, but other than that, there wasn't a whole lot to it. However, Jenny had always felt like it was so much more than just a place to get a sandwich or necessities. It felt like a comfortable meeting place.

It was owned by a friendly older Mennonite

couple who had learned her name after she'd been in their store just one time.

Frank and Carolyn Burns were in their early sixties and stocked just about everything anybody would ever need in their small, packed store. It was always crowded, too. Far more crowded than the bigger, newer supercenter located on the other side of Munfordville.

Jenny was sure people frequented it because Frank and Carolyn treated everyone who walked through the doors like old friends instead of paying customers. She'd certainly felt that way from the first time she'd visited.

The moment she walked in and the leather strap of sleigh bells hanging from the door handle jingled, Mr. Frank looked up from the cigarettes he was stocking behind the counter and smiled her way. "It's Miss Jenny Hilty!" he said. "I'm glad to see you."

Walking up to the counter, she smiled right back. "It's *gut* to see you, too, Mr. Frank."

"What brings you in today?"

"Milk."

"Want me to go grab you a gallon of two percent?"

"*Nah.* I'm going to look around for a few minutes, first."

He winked. "Gotcha. Take your time." Lowering his voice, he said, "You might want to take a gander over in aisle four."

Curious as to what he was referring to, Jenny walked there and then felt herself start blushing furiously. There was Cole Woods, standing smack in the middle of the aisle. Cole not only worked part-time for the grocer, he was one of her new friends. He looked over at her in surprise when she appeared.

"Hey, Jenny," he said. "You need something?"

She wasn't sure if he was teasing her or not. Wishing she could think of something remotely interesting to say, she shook her head. *"Nah. Nothing here."*

A little of the light that had been shining in his eyes dimmed. "Oh."

Great. Now he probably thought she was being mean on purpose. "I meant that I only came here for milk."

"Huh." He pushed his thick glasses up on the bridge of his nose. "Milk is in the dairy section."

"I know."

Jenny was glad about that. Though she didn't know Cole real well, she liked him. They were about the same age. She guessed he was maybe one year older than her, probably fifteen, since he was already done with school. He'd been really nice to her the first time she'd joined some of the other kids in the area for a Sunday-night singing. She'd been so nervous! She'd desperately wanted to fit in.

But though she always felt a little fluttery when

she was around him, Jenny wasn't sure that they would ever be more than just friends.

Another guy had also been really nice to her lately, and he was older and more mature.

Trying to fill in the silence, she mumbled, "I was just wandering around."

"If you have some extra time, do you want to go with me to the Millers' *haus* for a while? They have a litter of kittens. They're all different colors and really cute."

"*Danke*, but I better not. I should be getting home."

"Because your family is waiting on that milk."

"Yeah," she said quickly. "Well, I mean, it's something like that. See ya."

"Oh, yeah. Sure. Well, bye, Jenny."

Abruptly, she turned, claimed the gallon of two-percent milk from the dairy section, then carried it to the counter.

Mr. Frank raised his brows. "Checking out already? You didn't look around too long, little lady."

"I know."

"Didn't you go down aisle four?"

"I did, but I don't have as much time to shop or talk as I thought."

After he took her money, he slipped the plastic jug in a paper sack and placed her change on the counter. "Thanks for stopping in, Miss Jenny. See you soon."

"Sure thing. Bye."

She scurried out of there before she felt any guiltier about not staying longer to talk to Cole.

Just as she turned the corner, she saw the other person who had been occupying her thoughts. Shane McGovern. He was in the hardware store parking lot, putting something in the back of his white pickup truck. She slowed her steps, glad that he was occupied so he couldn't see her staring.

He was everything she shouldn't be interested in. He was older. Probably twenty-two, maybe even twenty-three. He was English, and he was also a bit slick. He talked fast and his gaze constantly looked around, like he was searching for something he couldn't quite locate.

He was also handsome. And when he stared at her, he made her feel like she was important and special. He listened to her, too. He was always asking her questions about her life and her family, as if he really cared.

Realizing that she'd been staring at him for a good couple of minutes, she ducked her head, intending to walk on by, but suddenly he looked up and waved a hand. "Hey, Jenny. Wait a sec, would you?"

A lady who had been standing next to him eyed Jenny curiously, then stopped and watched as Shane slammed the tailgate on his truck and trotted over to her.

As he crossed the street, Jenny tried to appear calm and collected, though she feared she probably failed at that terribly. It seemed she had no modesty where he was concerned.

"Hi, Shane," she said as she watched him approach. Today, he was wearing faded jeans, a knit T-shirt that fit him so tight she figured it could have been painted on, and thick-soled boots. He was tan, had earrings in his ears, and had blond hair that curled at the ends.

He was muscular and strong and supremely confident. He was her guilty crush. He was also everything her parents didn't want her to associate with and her uptight older sister would warn her against.

But maybe that was why she liked being around him so much?

"What are you up to today?" he asked as he came to a stop right next to her.

"I had to get some milk."

"Ah. Are you in a hurry to get home?"

"Not so much." Surely her milk would be fine for a while? "What about you?"

"That's the good thing about working for myself. I can decide when and where I want to work. How about I put that milk in my truck and we go for a walk?"

"Sure," she said nervously. This was the first time he was actually rearranging his schedule for her. That had to mean he thought she was really special, didn't it? "I can't walk for too long, though," she said quickly.

"How about just an hour, then?"

She nodded.

"Good girl." Holding out a hand, he said, "Give me your milk and I'll put it in my truck. Then we can go." He smiled again. "And while we walk, you can tell me all about what you've been up to. And what your family has been doing, too."

"All right," she promised. As she watched him cross the street again, it occurred to her that he always asked her questions, yet she still wasn't exactly sure what he did.

Maybe today, she'd ask some questions, too.

"Want to go for a walk in the woods?" he asked, pointing to an old trailhead that Cole had told her no one liked to use.

"Sure, but I heard it's overgrown with weeds."

"Weeds are a small price to pay for having you all to myself, Jenny."

Her heart felt as if it was melting. Obviously, Shane really liked her!

Pushing her misgivings aside, she followed him to the woods. She deserved to have some fun in her life. It wasn't her fault that her older sister had such bad taste in men and that her parents had just thrown the worst news possible at her.

If Jenny tried hard enough, she could pretend that none of that was happening and she was only just a girl, and that Shane thought she was unique and special.

And if he thought that, then she could pretend that nothing else mattered. Nothing but that moment with him.

Chapter 7

Monday evening, July 11

Taking a deep breath, Isaac knocked on the front door of the Hiltys' home and prepared himself to spend the next thirty minutes feeling worse than dirt.

After Mrs. Hilty answered the door and looked at him curiously instead of asking him in, he knew his expectations were right. "Isaac, may I help you with something?"

He folded his hands behind his back. "I was wondering if I might be able to talk to Hannah for a few moments."

"Hannah?"

She looked so surprised, he now felt even more ill at ease. Either Hannah never got visitors or she had mentioned his insensitive remarks.

"*Jah.*" Hating how his voice squeaked, he cleared his throat. "I mean, yes, I came to pay her a call. Is she here?"

"She is." She smiled apologetically. "I'm sorry,

I guess I didn't expect for her to be receiving any callers. Come in and sit down in the living room."

Now this was worse than bad. Mrs. Hilty was getting the completely wrong impression of why he'd shown up. He didn't dare correct her, though. The last thing he wanted to do was embarrass Hannah.

Entering the small room that only held a small couch, two chairs, and two side tables, Mrs. Hilty said, "I'll go tell Hannah you are here. I'll be right back."

"Thank you."

When he was alone, he took a better look around the room. The furniture seemed new and it was well made. Not cheap by any standard. That surprised him. Their house was nice enough, but on the small side. He'd gotten the impression from Ben that they didn't have a lot of extra money. Not for furniture like he was sitting on. Though it didn't matter to him if they had money or not, he realized that he'd made yet another quick assumption about Hannah and her family.

When he looked toward the hall to see if Mrs. Hilty was on her way back, he was startled to spy Hannah walking toward him.

Today, she had on a light-green dress with long sleeves. Everything about her looked serene and calm. Except for her eyes. They looked as turbulent and troubled as he'd ever seen them.

"Hi, Isaac," she said hesitantly. "My mother said you wanted to speak to me?"

"*Jah.*" Realizing that she was standing while he was still sitting, he got to his feet. "Want to sit down?" he asked, knowing he sounded as awkward as he felt. When she didn't move, he rushed on. "This won't take long."

"All right." At last she sat, but she didn't even bother to hide her feelings. It looked like she would rather be anywhere else.

He didn't blame her; he knew the feeling.

"Well?" she prodded.

"I wanted to apologize to you for how I acted the other day." Looking at her earnestly, he continued. "I sounded like a jerk and I should have been more welcoming. Definitely more understanding."

"Understanding?"

"*Jah.* On account of all you've been through."

Her eyes narrowed. "What, exactly, have I been through?"

That lump appeared back in his throat. Somehow, he'd just made a mess of things. "Well, you know," he said weakly. How, exactly, was he supposed to mention something that she probably hadn't wanted to talk about in the first place?

"*Nee.* I'm afraid I do not."

How was he to handle this now? Feeling like he was in the middle of a train wreck, but seeing no other way to go, he kept talking. "I talked to your brother the other day. When he was over at our house. With Samuel. I mean Sam."

"Yes?"

"And he told us about why your family moved here. The *real* reason." When she stared at him, her expression carefully blank, he took a deep breath. This was awful! "You know."

She exhaled. "You mean because an Englisher was stalking me? Taking pictures of me?" Her voice turned sharper. "How it's my fault we had to move because he was lurking outside our house and taking photographs of me through my bedroom window?"

He'd felt sorry for her, but now he was shocked. "I didn't know all that."

She sat up straighter. "What? Ben didn't tell you everything about my personal life?"

"Well, um . . ."

"Did he tell you what you needed to know? Or maybe there are other details you are curious about?"

"*Nee*—" He was mentally squirming now. If only there was a way to start this conversation again!

Hands clasped in her lap, she spoke quietly. "*Danke* for coming over. I appreciate your apology. You may go now."

Maybe the right thing to do would be to leave. But he couldn't.

Hannah Hilty wasn't a stranger. She wasn't

someone he might never see again. She was his neighbor, and he wanted to one day be her friend. She'd also been through too much to only know the worst of him.

He felt bad. He also felt a little irritated. After all, people misspoke all the time. Couldn't she try to be even a little bit more understanding? "Look, I know I made a mistake. But I came over here to do the right thing. I came over to apologize."

"And you wanted to do that because of my past."

"No, because it was the right thing to do," he countered. Getting to his feet, he said, "I know I could have handled things better."

When he saw that her expression hadn't changed, he started pacing. "Maybe I should have never mentioned what your brother said. Maybe I should have pretended that I didn't know about your past. Maybe that would have been better. That said, I, well, I think you are making a real mistake by refusing to listen to me." When he saw her mutinous expression flicker, he added, "I'm not perfect, but I'm sure not as bad as you are making me out to be."

Just as he started to turn to cross the room again, Hannah got to her feet.

"Isaac, stop, please."

He did as she asked but didn't turn around. It was probably wrong, but he didn't want to see even more hurt and accusation shining in her eyes.

"You're right," she said. "You came over here to make amends and I've been nothing but judgmental and rude. I'm sorry that I've been so mean."

When he turned to face her, he saw true remorse etched in her features. "It's okay."

"I don't know what's wrong with me," she stated, looking like she was as confused as he felt. "I seem to be a different person than I was before. I used to be happier, carefree. Braver, maybe."

"What happened changed you."

"*Jah.* It did. I had thought a new place, new people, a new life would make the memories easier to handle, but the opposite is true. Now I can't help but dwell on the memories. I don't have anything to take the place of them."

He noticed again how pretty she was. Dark hair, unusual light-hazel eyes. A straight, finely crafted nose. High cheekbones. She had an almost exotic look to her, so different than most of the Amish girls' looks that he was familiar with. He realized why he was reacting so strongly to her. He thought she was beautiful.

And now that he knew a small part of her history, he felt protective over her, too. He wanted to help her. He wanted to be someone she could trust, to depend on.

It didn't make sense, but he'd learned years ago that few things did. Their lives were in the Lord's hands, after all.

"I didn't just come over here to apologize. I also

wanted to tell you about a charity event that a group of people our age is putting together. It's a sandwich sale."

Her eyes brightened. "Really? Those sales are fun."

He smiled back, glad they had done those types of fund-raising back in Berlin, too. "They're real popular in Hart County. People bring ham and turkey, cheese, pickles, and other sandwich fixings, and get together to make dozens of sandwiches." One time, he remembered, his mother made over a hundred to help a family whose barn had been lost in a tornado.

"What are people making sandwiches for?" Hannah asked.

"Darryl and Mercy Gingerich. Their new baby was born with a heart defect. She needs surgery." Feeling better now that he was talking about something he felt more comfortable with, he added, "There's going to be about a dozen of us working on this, most of them our age. We're going to sell not only sandwiches but bags of chips, homemade pies and whoopee pies, and jars of freshly brewed tea and lemonade." He paused, giving her a moment to absorb everything he'd said. "Will you join us?"

She opened her mouth, seemed to hesitate, then nodded. "That sounds like a lot of fun. *Danke*."

"I'm glad."

Hannah smiled slightly. "You are right, Isaac.

The best cure for dwelling on bad memories is to make some new ones. Working on a sandwich sale sounds like great fun. Thank you for asking me."

"Our first meeting is in two days, on Wednesday. Are you free? Will you go there with me?"

"*Jah*. I will."

When he met her eyes, he couldn't resist smiling. Especially when she smiled right back.

Chapter 8

Wednesday, July 13

The first meeting for the sandwich sale was at a home on the outskirts of Munfordville. Sitting by Isaac's side as he drove his buggy, Hannah was a bundle of nerves. She still had a difficult time around large groups of people. She also didn't want to make a bad impression on Isaac's friends.

Just as she was about to ask him about the couple hosting the party, Isaac pulled the brake on the buggy. "We're here."

Turning to gaze at the yard, she practically gasped. It was that pretty.

Situated in at least one full acre, a large white house stood proudly next to a prosperous-looking garden. On its other side was an old stone and wood barn with a shiny tin roof. Numerous flower beds filled with blooming tulips and daffodils were freshly mulched.

At least eight dresses hung on the clothesline that ran from the house to a tall white post on the edge of the garden. The dresses were of varying sizes and colors. Their vibrant shades of raspberry, plum, royal blue, and meadow green made the grass underneath them look greener and the sky above look brighter.

It all looked so tranquil and perfect, Hannah couldn't help but sigh. She'd always hoped to have a lovely home like this one day.

"It's pretty. Ain't so?" Isaac asked as he parked his horse and buggy near the entrance next to at least five other buggies.

Hannah nodded as she hopped down. "It's charming." She tapped a foot on the limestone walkway that led from the widest section of the driveway to the front door of the house. "This walkway is so pretty, too."

"You'll find that lots of homes here in Munfordville and Horse Cave make good use of all the limestone that lays underground. It's certainly plentiful around here."

"I love how different this house is from most of the other buildings in Berlin. It's so warm and welcoming, yet cozy."

Looking down at her, he smiled. "I think you're going to find that Karen and John are just as warm and welcoming as their home."

The front door opened right as they approached it. Two women about her age filled the doorway.

"We wondered when you were going to get here," a woman with a face full of freckles said.

"Have you been waiting to start because of us?" Isaac asked.

"Of course not. You know Paul and Aaron haven't arrived yet."

"I didn't think they had. I didn't see their horse." Turning to Hannah, Isaac grinned. "Paul and Aaron are always late. They can't seem to help it."

"We don't fault them too much, though," a man who walked up behind the two women said. "They always bring food with them. Usually, something they prepared in their smoker."

Hannah chuckled. "I've found those are the best kinds of guests to have over."

When the group at the door smiled at her, she felt Isaac's approval slip over her like a warm shawl. "Hannah, this is Maggie, John, and Christina. Everyone, this is my new neighbor, Hannah Hilty."

The group stepped back so Isaac and Hannah could enter. Then they gathered around them like a litter of eager puppies. "You're from Ohio, *jah*?" Maggie asked.

"*Jah*. Berlin," Hannah replied.

"You'll have much in common with Darryl and Mercy, then. They are originally from that area. From Charm, I think."

"I'll be eager to meet them."

"Now, tell us about you," Maggie said as they walked into a large great room that was filled with seven or eight other people. "Do you work?"

"*Nee*. Not right now. I did back in Berlin. I worked as a server at a restaurant. Now I am helping my brother and sister with their schoolwork."

"I help out with my family, too."

"Maggie will do that . . . until she and Paul get married," Christina said in a high, singsong voice.

Hannah clasped her hands together. "Oh, you're engaged! Congratulations!"

"We're marrying in four months," Maggie said, her voice giddy. "I can hardly believe it. I'm excited, but there are so many details to take care of first. I don't know if I'll get them all done."

"It's going to be beautiful," Christina said.

Maggie looked at Christina fondly. "She has to say that, I think. She's my cousin and matron of honor."

The girls' giddiness instantly relaxed Hannah. Weddings and wedding plans were something all Amish girls had in common. "What are your colors?"

Isaac pressed a hand on her arm. "I'm going to go talk with the men while you ladies discuss wedding things."

"Okay. *Danke*, Isaac," she said shyly, realizing he'd been hovering by her side until he was sure that she was comfortable.

When he and Joe left, Christina eyed her a little more closely. "Are you and Isaac courting?"

"Oh, *nee*. He is just being kind. I, well, I was a little nervous about joining in today."

Christina nodded. "I would feel the same way. It's hard being new. We only moved here two years ago. We came from southern Kentucky, though. Maybe we had an easier time adjusting because we didn't move as far." Smiling at Maggie, she said, "Plus, we were moving near family."

"Maybe so."

The conversation continued. Christina and Maggie took her around and introduced her to the other people who were there.

Some of them she'd met before at church, others were part of a different church district.

Hannah kept waiting for someone to mention how reclusive she'd been, but no one said anything unkind. She wondered if they simply hadn't noticed that she hadn't been around or were too polite to mention it.

Instead, they swept her up in conversation that was much like the ones she used to share with Kirsten and her other friends back in Berlin. They talked of weddings and siblings, of work and food and diets, and the men there.

After another ten minutes passed, the door opened again and the elusive Aaron and Paul entered, much to Maggie's obvious delight. Then she and Christina led everyone into the dining room, where a whole variety of dishes were set out for them to enjoy.

Tiny sandwiches filled with roast beef shared platters with ham and Swiss cheese. There were potato, fruit, and noodle salads. Cookies and meatballs, too. When Hannah took a plate and joined in the line, Isaac returned to her side.

"Hi, again," she teased.

"I glanced over at you a couple of times," he said with a smile. "Each time, you were in conversation with someone. Since it looked like you are doing all right, I decided to give you a little space."

She was touched that he'd been so concerned about how she was doing. It was so sweet, especially given the rocky way their previous conversations had been.

"Everyone is nice. I'm glad I came," she said quietly. "Thank you for bringing me."

"No need to thank me. I'm just glad you said yes," he said as they moved forward. "Everyone seems to like you, Hannah. I think you're going to make some friends here."

"I think so, too." She smiled before spearing a couple of meatballs and putting them on her plate.

When everyone had their plates filled, Maggie directed them all back into the great room. After everyone got settled, Maggie bowed her head in silent prayer. The others followed suit.

As she closed her eyes, Hannah gave thanks for the food and the hands that prepared it. Then added her own private prayer of gratitude for the Lord guiding her to be a part of the group. She'd needed this. With some surprise, she realized that she'd been here almost an hour and had never once felt scared or had dwelled on Trent or the past.

She was making progress, and she was certainly grateful for that.

"The first thing we need to do," Maggie's fiancé, Paul, announced, "is to set a date and a goal for the auction. Anyone have a date in mind?"

"I talked to Darryl before I came over," a man from the other side of the room said. "Their *boppli* is struggling and was in and out of the hospital just last week. I think they're going to need any help we can give them as soon as possible."

"Let's get busy, then," Aaron said.

Maggie scanned all the faces of the people who had gathered. "Is putting all this together in two weeks crazy?"

"Ah, yes," Joe said. "We need to make flyers, order everything, and clear our schedules."

Maggie nodded. "You have a point. What about

three weeks, then? I know it will be hard, but Eli has a point. The Gingerich family needs our help now."

Hannah couldn't believe it, but she realized she was actually holding her breath to hear what everyone was going to say. In just an hour's time, she'd become emotionally invested in Mercy and Darryl's struggles.

Though she was sorry for their baby, she was grateful to have the opportunity to push aside her own troubles and concentrate on someone else.

"I think three weeks is possible," Isaac called out from his seat right next to Hannah. "Remember, everyone, it's many hands that make projects like this successful. That means no one has to bear the brunt of this project alone."

Paul nodded, a smile playing on his lips. "You're right, Isaac." Looking at the calendar, he called out a date. "This is when we'll be holding the sale, come rain or come shine."

Joe stood up. "I have a second cousin who teaches at the high school. I'll talk to her to make sure we can hold it in the high school parking lot."

"*Danke*, Joe," Maggie said. Turning to the rest of the group, she said, "I made a chart with all the types of jobs I could think of. Before everyone leaves, please sign up on the poster board."

"*Danke*, Maggie. And thank you, everyone, for jumping in with both feet. This sandwich sale is going to be wonderful. Wonderful-*gut*!"

The room erupted in applause while several people cheered and added their thanks.

When it died down, Isaac turned Hannah's way with a grin. "This is mighty exciting. Do you want to work on something together?"

Hannah nodded. "Since you are pretty much the only person I know well, I am going to say yes. You're stuck with me."

"I'm okay with that. I'm thinking that there are worse things to be stuck with."

Hannah smiled, feeling more and more pleased about how things were going between them.

Thirty minutes later, she stood by his side as they stared at Maggie's chart.

"I don't want to do anything with advertising or selling," she shyly admitted. "Is that okay with you?"

Isaac didn't seem surprised. "That's fine. How about we work the day before the sandwich making? That involves going to different houses, picking up ingredients, and bringing everything to the place where the production line will be."

"*Jah*. I can do that."

"Do you like to bake?" Maggie asked. "We can always use help making cookies and brownies."

Hannah noticed that Maggie had offered choices. Women could sign up to make several dozen cookies by themselves or join in the group effort to assemble the sandwiches together. Taking a leap, Hannah pointed to the group activity. "I'll work here, too."

"And I'll help sell, too," Isaac said.

Maggie clapped her hands together. "It's good of you to volunteer for that position. If you didn't, I would have put you there myself." Winking at Hannah, she explained, "Isaac has kind of a big mouth, you see."

"I'm starting to notice that." Feeling lighter than she had in weeks, Hannah added, "It's a good thing, though. Especially when it comes to selling."

"I aim to sell at least a hundred sandwiches on my own. That will show my parents that my penchant for talking is good for something," Isaac quipped.

Hannah was still excited about the afternoon's meeting when they got back in his buggy another hour later.

"This was fun," she said when they stopped at the foot of her driveway. "I'm so glad you asked me to go."

"I'm glad you did. Like I said earlier, you made a big impression on everyone. People like you, Hannah."

"I liked your friends, too."

"The next gathering is in three days. Want to go together again?"

"I do."

"Great. I'll see you then, if not before." He

tipped his hat slightly in her direction before motioning his horse forward.

Hoping to make the euphoric feeling last a little longer, she watched Isaac's buggy disappear around the bend.

Then, with her mind filled with plans and stories to share with her mother, she headed up the driveway toward the house.

Still thinking about the meeting, she almost didn't notice the potted plants that had appeared out of nowhere just a few days before.

Someone had neatly snipped all the heads of the daisies off. Discarded blooms lay scattered all around the ground. Some of the flowers' petals were already wilting and shriveling up.

Just like that, the momentary burst of hope that had been inside of her fizzled into nothing.

Chapter 9

Wednesday, July 13

Hannah didn't say a word about the desecrated daisies to her family. She was afraid they would act as if she was making much of nothing.

But she was rattled. The appearance of both the daisies and their later ruin were signs that her troubles with Trent weren't over. Now a dull sense of foreboding filled her. She was going to have to deal with him again. She hoped she would be strong enough.

And if the daisies weren't a sign that Trent was stalking her again? What if she was exaggerating everything? What if she was imagining trouble where there was none? Well, that was just as disturbing.

Hannah felt more alone than ever before. Her parents had other, more pressing concerns to focus on than her fears. And her siblings already resented her. Hannah didn't want to give Ben and Jenny even more reasons to not want to be around her.

She hoped she wasn't slowly losing her mind.

But she worried that she was.

Feeling as if her head was about to burst, Hannah trudged down the hall to her room. Glad that Jenny wasn't there so she'd have a few minutes to herself, she sat down on her bed and wrote a long letter to Kirsten. She was so thankful that they remained so close.

Though they hadn't been corresponding with great regularity, they were still writing to each other and sharing much of what they were experiencing day to day.

Kirsten had written Hannah several letters talking about her feelings for Henry, her neighbor. By turns she would either be longing for Henry to pay more attention to her, or complaining about his attention while being unsure if she was ready to commit to him.

Hannah had responded to Kirsten's concerns again and again. Never once did she convey that she was out of patience with Kirstin's rocky love life or thought Kirsten should make up her mind.

Because of that, Hannah had no worries about being completely honest with her best friend.

She wrote and wrote. Told about the sudden, *real* reason that her parents had wanted to move. Told about how Ben and Jenny seemed determined to resent her. She confided to Kirsten about Isaac and how their rocky start had blossomed into a new friendship.

Haltingly, Hannah even confided that she was sure that Isaac was becoming someone she was learning to trust. She also shared how grateful she was about this. Hannah had feared that she'd been pretty sure that she would never want to trust another man ever again.

Finally, in closing, she told Kirsten about the appearance of the daisies.

She wrote:

Don't you think them being here is odd?

Every time I look at them, I feel sick to my stomach. I want to pick up those pots and throw them into the woods across the house. I would, too, if I thought no one in my house would notice.

But everyone here only seems to notice all

of my odd behaviors. If I started doing something like that, they would resent me even more.

Please tell me about what I should do next. You are pretty much the only person I trust now, Kirsten.

Feeling satisfied that she'd conveyed all of the events as completely as possible, Hannah quickly sealed the letter in an envelope and neatly wrote out Kirsten's address, then left it for the postal worker.

When she trotted down the driveway, she did her best to ignore the daisies littering the ground.

She almost succeeded.

Sunday, July 17

On Sunday, after the preacher closed the service with one final prayer, Hannah was anxious to move around.

She was still so rattled by those daisies, she couldn't seem to focus on anything else. When she saw Maggie and Isaac and several other people who she'd met at the meetings, Hannah felt her anxiety creep up.

What if she had misjudged how friendly everyone had been?

Instead of taking a chance on ruining her new friendships, Hannah thought the right thing to do would be to go home and curl up with a good book.

She told her parents that she was going to skip the luncheon and head back home early.

Her mind was so woozy, she was sure if she talked to one of the new friends she'd made at the gathering, she would say the absolute wrong thing and mess up a good first impression.

"You really want to walk home on your own?" Daed asked, looking worried. "Do you think that is wise?"

"Our home is less than two miles away, and it's only two right turns. Plus, it's a sunny day out. I'll be fine."

Her mother leaned closer. "What is going on? I thought you enjoyed yourself yesterday at the meeting."

"I did, Mamm." Feeling trapped, she added, "Please, just let me go."

Though she still looked worried, her mother backed off. "Of course. We'll see you later, then."

"Thanks." After giving her another weak smile, she darted toward the driveway.

"Hannah? Hannah, wait," Isaac called out. When he reached her side, he looked at her curiously. "Where are ya going?"

"I decided to go home early."

"Now? Are you walking by yourself?"

"I am." He sounded so incredulous, she was tempted to smile. Instead, she simply looked at him, hoping she looked much calmer than she felt.

But Isaac still looked concerned. "It's kind of a long walk. And I don't know if it's all that safe."

"I don't think I'll run into another person. I'll be perfectly safe." As safe as she could be with only her private thoughts, that is.

Hannah could see that he was debating whether or not to offer to walk by her side. She decided to make his choice easier.

"To be honest, I was hoping to have some time alone right now."

"Why do you need time alone? Is anything the matter?"

If they were closer, she would have told him about the daisies. But they weren't. "Everything is fine." Because she was so stressed, her voice turned sharp. "There is nothing wrong with a woman wanting to take a walk by herself, you know."

His dark eyes clouded with hurt. "I didn't say there was. Hey, is something wrong? You seem a little different than you did yesterday."

"Everything is fine, Isaac. I just think I should be able to go for a walk without having to explain myself."

"I'm not trying to make you do that."

She didn't want to fight with him. "Look, you better go get in line before the food is all gone."

His expression turned blank. "Sure. Yeah. All right."

Though she privately wondered what she was doing, Hannah started out again. She stayed on the road but stayed close to the side, passing overgrown hedges and patches of hollyhocks dotted with bright yellow wildflowers. Their fragrance permeated the air, infusing it with a sharp, sweet tang. The scent was both familiar and foreign. It brought back memories of last summer, when she'd still been trying to decide if the mild anxiety she'd felt around Trent had any bearing on truth or if it had just been something she'd embellished in her mind.

Startled that she was yet, again, thinking about the man she'd been trying so hard to extinguish from her life, Hannah felt her stomach clench. Remembering what she'd read about calming anxiety in a book from the library, she began taking slow, deep breaths in order to relax her body.

Unfortunately, all that deep breathing seemed to do was cause her to inhale even more of the fragrant air and make those memories seem even more pronounced.

It was a difficult cycle, proving once again that she might have made great strides by being out in the world, but she truly only ever felt at peace when she was in the safety of an enclosed room with a sturdy lock on the door.

Irritated with herself, she picked up her pace. You are safe, Hannah, she chided herself. You are safe and have become your own worst problem. You don't need to look for people to be scared of, you are practically afraid of your own shadow!

Her irritation spurred her to walk even faster. She was close to running now. Each step pounding the hard asphalt underfoot, jarring her hips and knees. Causing a bit of discomfort.

But at least that slight pain felt wholesome and pure. It wasn't tainted by dark memories or shadowed by fears. Instead, it was easily brought on and all consuming.

Little by little, she stopped thinking about any-thing but walking home. She stopped seeing birds and plants or noticing the greenery or how the flowers perfumed the air. All she could think about was getting back to her room and closing her door tightly against the world.

That was why when she turned the corner and a twig snapped behind her, followed by a rustle of branches and leaves, she nearly screamed. Some-one was behind her.

Someone was following her and she hadn't even been aware of it.

She started to hyperventilate. The right, smart thing to do would be to turn around and alleviate her worries.

But if she did that, then she would know without a doubt who it was. If she did, she would have to deal with it. And if her worst fears were realized, if the person was actually Trent, she knew she might very well freeze and be at his mercy.

But she had to know. She had to. Feeling like a pair of wires were controlling the movement of her head, pushing and pulling her without any effort on her own, she looked behind her.

And saw her sister.

"Jenny, what are you doing here?" she asked.

"Trying to catch up with you," Jenny replied as she walked up. Looking irritated, she said, "Why were you walking so fast, anyway? It was like you were in a race or something."

"I don't know. I guess I started getting panicked about being by myself."

"Why? We're here in Kentucky. We're nowhere near Trent." Jenny crossed her arms in front of her chest, effectively putting up a barrier in between the two of them. And because there was already quite a wide figurative barrier, it seemed like her little sister had just taken two giant steps back from her.

Leaving her feeling even more alone.

She started walking again. "We don't know that for sure. He could have discovered where I was." She debated about whether or not to tell Jenny about the daisies appearing out of nowhere, and now the even more disturbing sight of the blooms scattered all about the ground. She didn't want to scare Jenny.

But as they continued to walk side by side,

Hannah noticed that her little sister didn't seem all that disturbed. Instead, she seemed to be doing her best to hold her tongue.

By the time they reached their short driveway, Hannah was out of patience with Jenny's attitude.

"Jenny, I'm tired of watching you acting like you're afraid to speak your mind. Just say whatever it is that you are thinking."

"You won't like hearing it."

"I'm sure I won't, but that doesn't matter," she replied as they started walking on the gravel. "I'd rather know what you are thinking than imagining it."

"All right." Jenny pursed her lips, seemed to gather her courage, then blurted, "I think you are being ridiculous. You must think the whole world is revolving around you."

Hannah had expected Jenny to be blunt, but her vehemence took her off guard. "I don't think that."

"Of course you do. You're acting like you're the prettiest girl around. As if Trent wasn't going to be able to stand that you moved away and followed you here."

"He didn't stalk me because he thought I was pretty, Jenny. I thought you understood what the police told Mamm and Daed and me. He was fixated on me for reasons of his own. It made no sense."

"You are what makes no sense."

"Because?"

"Because you are still wandering around scared of your own shadow." She waved a hand impatiently. "You act as if he is about to jump out at you from every corner."

"Of course I've been afraid," Hannah retorted. "I keep imagining that someone is watching me. Maybe he isn't. But I'm doing the best I can. Though it's hard when things like *this* happen—" She waved to the chopped-up daisies.

Jenny raised her eyebrows. "What things?"

"These!" When Jenny still looked confused, Hannah said, "You know Trent gave me daisies all the time. Just a couple of days ago, someone put them here. And now, look what someone did."

"What did they do?"

Hating that Jenny was not only sounding sarcastic but making her spell everything out, Hannah pointed to the daisy heads littering the ground. *"This,"* she said. "Look what he did. He cut them up."

Jenny laughed. It was a cruel, empty sound. "Trent didn't do that, I did."

"You?" Hannah knew her voice was weak and thready. "I don't understand. Why would you do something like that?"

Jenny looked away. "You were so worked up about those daisies, I decided to get rid of the blooms. Then they would just look like plain old green plants."

"But you didn't get rid of the blooms. Not really.

They are scattered around on the ground." An ugly thought occurred to her. "Did you want me to worry and get even more upset? Did you think that would be fun to see?"

"Of course not. I was going to sweep them up, then Daed asked me to help in the kitchen. I forgot all about them." She sighed. "Now that I know you got home safe, I'm going to go out for a while."

"Where are you going?"

Jenny tossed her head. "That is none of your business. But Mamm and Daed think I'm home with you. If they come home before I do, make up something about where I've been, okay?"

Hannah shook her head. "Of course I won't do that. If you are sneaking around, this is a problem. It's dangerous, too."

"Stop making up dangers where there aren't any!"

"I'm not—"

"Stop," Jenny interrupted. "You owe me, Hannah. I left everything I had for you. Now that I'm finally making friends, you are not going to take that away from me."

Hannah was so shocked, she simply gaped at Jenny as she walked back down the road, this time toward town.

She'd hoped their lives would get easier when they moved to Kentucky, but so far it seemed like everything was just getting more mixed up and hard to understand.

Chapter 10

On Monday morning, Isaac was still revisiting the last conversation he'd shared with Hannah. Working in his shop at the front of their property, he found himself analyzing each word they'd said and Hannah's reactions to each.

This was a rarity for him. For better or worse, he was mostly the type of man who only looked forward. It had helped him when he was recovering from his bout with meningitis. It had also aided him during other times of stress or worry.

Again and again, he'd found that it had done no good to try to analyze why things happened or dwell on what-ifs. It was far better to simply leave the whys and why-nots up to the Lord and look toward each day in a positive way.

But then again, he had never met anyone like Hannah. She was prickly and tentative. Those qualities made him want to try harder to please her.

Then, by turns, she would tease and joke and make him wonder if he'd simply exaggerated her tentativeness in his mind.

Realizing that his head was drifting away from work yet again, Isaac gave up on refinishing the pine dining room table and pulled out his broom and dust mop. Since he couldn't seem to make peace with his state of mind, it was probably best to simply clean.

The last thing he wanted to do was ruin a piece of furniture that he was being paid good money to refurbish.

"I've got your dinner, Isaac," his mother called out as she walked through the doorway, Spot trotting inside by her side.

"*Danke*," he said as he leaned down to give his dog a pat on the head. "I could use a break, and some company."

"Spot was staring at the front door, pining for you. I figured you wouldn't mind his company."

"Not at all."

While he knelt down to pet his dog again, Mamm looked around the room with obvious surprise. "You're cleaning today?"

"I am." He picked up his broom again as Spot went to his favorite place in the back corner of his work space.

A line formed between her brows as she scanned the area. "This isn't like you. You are usually hard at work on new projects on Mondays. Are you expecting a visitor or a new client?"

"*Nee*." Leaning both hands on the top of his broom handle, he tried to give an explanation that she would easily accept. "It was time to get organized. You know how hard of a time I have working on pieces if there is clutter around me."

She smirked. "Um, no. I don't think that's it. You love to work on your furniture. Why, sometimes I think a storm could go through these hills and you wouldn't even be aware of it until you walked outside." Looking at him carefully, she said, "*Nee*, something is going on with you and it's not a sudden desire for cleanliness."

Unable to refute his mother's assessment, he laughed. "All right. You caught me. The truth is that I can't seem to concentrate today. I decided it was safer to clean instead of risking the furniture."

"What has your mind in knots?"

"Nothing I care to share." He held out a hand. "Thank you for the lunch, though. I am thankful for it."

She waved off his thanks with an impatient hand. "Isaac, you know I am not going to leave you like this." Walking over to his now spotlessly clean workbench, she set the basket on it and started setting out a plate filled with country fried steak, corn, and some pickled beets. "Here. You sit down and I'll help you work through whatever it is that's bothering you."

"It ain't that easy, Mamm. I don't have a problem I'm trying to solve. It's just something that's been occupying my brain."

"I have a feeling this 'thing' has hazel eyes and dark hair."

"Maybe."

"I thought you enjoyed your time with her on Saturday."

"I did."

"Then, what's the problem?"

"Hannah seemed like a completely different person yesterday. She took off for home directly after services. She didn't even stay for the meal afterward."

"That's too bad, but you shouldn't bring anything into it. She probably just wanted to get home and do chores or something."

"I would have thought that, too, but she just seemed so distant. I think it was something else. Maybe something to do with the real reason they moved."

"You mean with the story her brother shared?"

He nodded. "She's so timid. I don't want to scare her. And yet, I am not sure if I should be thinking about her in any way other than trying to be her friend."

"Isaac, there's no reason for you to be rushing into a relationship. You always want to jump ahead and worry about things that are three or four steps away. You know that's a difficult road. Things happen. Life happens. Perhaps you should simply just enjoy the moment."

"That's good advice." But it was also hard to take. "Do you think I should visit her again? We are supposed to go to another meeting soon. Should I wait until then?"

"I'm not sure. She might not want to talk about something serious before the meeting. But if you don't mention your concerns, she might think you don't care."

"Exactly. That's why I've been cleaning. I think this is all something that I need to figure out on my own."

"I'll try to help if I can."

"And I'll be glad for your help . . . unless it's a problem of the heart."

She laughed. "You've got me there."

"Thank you for bringing me lunch, Mamm. I appreciate it."

"You are welcome." Wagging a finger playfully, she added, "Now, don't forget to eat."

"I won't." He picked up his fork for good measure. The moment she walked out, he put the utensil back down. There was no way he was going to be able to eat until he figured out how he was going to handle his feelings about that girl.

It was simply too bad that neither choice seemed like the right choice to make.

The local library had turned out to be a pretty good place for Jenny and Ben to work on their assignments. There were other people around, and sometimes other teenagers that she met at church.

It was also close to A&L, so Jenny could say hello to Mr. or Mrs. Burns or meet some of their new friends.

But even though the location for the studies had improved a lot, she and Ben were still stuck doing a bunch of work neither of them wanted to do.

"It seems pretty dumb that we're studying about countries that we'll never see," Ben grumbled under his breath. "Hannah gives us the dumbest assignments."

Looking up from the map she'd been attempting to color code, Jenny agreed. "We should have told Mamm and Daed that we wanted to go to the Amish school instead of letting Hannah tutor us. At least then we'd have friends to talk to about all this work."

Ben scratched his chin. "You're right. Do you think it's too late to do that?"

"For me, it is. I'm almost done with school forever."

"I wish I was." Ben groaned. "There's no way I want to do school alone with Hannah next year."

Jenny knew she'd hate that. "It's not too late for you. Tell Mamm and Daed that you want to attend the Amish school. They'd let you go."

Ben's eyes lit up with hope. "You think?"

"Oh, yeah. Mamm is working all the time. Nowadays, she don't care what you do as long as she doesn't have to deal with it. Just tell Daed."

"I'm going to." Sounding much happier, he added, "I could be with Sam and all his friends. That would be much better than sitting here."

Jenny smiled at him. "Let me know if you want me to talk to Mamm and Daed for you."

"*Danke.*"

"No problem. Anything has got to be better than working with Hannah all the time."

"That sounds kind of mean. She ain't doing that bad of a job anymore."

"You're right. She's not," Jenny grudgingly agreed. "But even so, lessons at the kitchen table can't replace a real school."

Looking hesitant, Ben said, "Hey, Jenny, do you like Hannah at all anymore?"

"I like her fine." Of course, she felt her cheeks heating. "I guess I've been pretty mean to her lately."

"I realized how badly I was acting when I was talking to Sam's family about Trent." He blew out a gust of air. "When I said it all out loud and had seen their reactions, I realized I haven't been very understanding to Hannah. I feel bad about that."

"I can't believe you told them about Trent. Why did you, in the first place?"

"Sam's brother Isaac was acting like Hannah didn't have a reason to be so skittish around other people. It made me mad. I mean, he shouldn't talk that way about our sister! That's when I told Sam and Isaac what happened."

"Wow."

He nodded. "*Jah.* Jenny, they both stared at me with shocked expressions. Horrified ones. That's when I realized how inconsiderate I've been." Moving closer to Jenny, he said, "For weeks, I didn't even think about how she had to move away from all of her friends, too. I was only thinking about myself."

Jenny was starting to feel pretty guilty, too. "You shouldn't feel bad. You can't help how you feel."

"Maybe not, but I'm learning that I can help how I act. Ain't so?"

"I guess so." Just as she was about to share what she'd told Hannah on the way home from church, she saw Cole walking toward them. "Hi," she said with a smile.

"You know Cole, too?"

She was just going to ask how he knew Cole when he smiled at them both.

"Hiya. What are you two doing at the library?"

"Studying," Ben said with a groan. "What about you?"

"Returning a couple of my little brother's books." After adjusting the bridge of his rims up a bit, he added, "He really likes to read."

"That's nice of you to take care of his books for him."

Cole shrugged. "He's only seven. It ain't like he can take care of things on his own now. Plus, he's my brother."

His easy explanation shamed her. It was like looking in a mirror and suddenly seeing a flaw she hadn't known existed. She'd been so sure all along that she was misunderstood—but it seemed she'd forgotten that *everyone* had responsibilities and obligations.

That everything wasn't just about her and what she wanted.

Smiling at him, Jenny asked, "Do you want to sit with me for a while? Ben was going to go home soon."

Ben coughed. "I was?"

She stared at him pointedly. "You just said you were. Don't ya remember?"

"Oh, yeah." He started stacking his notebook and library books together. "I almost forgot that I had to hurry home."

"Sorry you can't stay," Cole said politely.

"That means that after we are done here, you could maybe walk me home . . . if it isn't too far out of your way."

Cole's ears turned red. "*Danke*, but I should probably not walk you anywhere."

"Why not?"

"Because you are seeing that Englisher. Shane, right?" Not exactly looking at her in the eye, he said, "He isn't very nice. Um, I don't think he is the sort who would take my walking you around in the dark kindly. At all."

Ben loosened his grip on his books and sat back down. Looking both confused and increasingly agitated, he stared at Jenny. "Who is Shane?"

Feeling both of the boys' glares fixated on her, Jenny shifted nervously. "Shane is no one you need to worry about."

"No, I think I do," Ben said. "Especially if you are keeping him a secret." Lowering his voice, he said, "Why would you sneak around like that, Jenny? Didn't what happened with Hannah teach you anything?"

"This is nothing like that. And I don't want to talk about Hannah and Trent."

"There is no Hannah and Trent. That was the problem." Looking angry, he added, "What's gotten into you?"

"Not a thing. I'm simply trying to live my life without having everyone second-guess every single thing I do."

"So you are seeing people behind everyone's back?"

"Ben, I really, really don't want to talk about this right now." Or ever.

"You haven't told your family that you've been stepping out with Shane?" Cole interjected, looking disturbed. "They don't know you're seeing someone so old?"

"How old is he?" Ben asked.

"None of your business," she told Ben. Turning to Cole, she straightened. "I didn't think I had to tell my parents everything anymore. I'm fourteen, you know."

"So. You should have told them," Ben said.

She glared at her brother. "I bet you can't wait to go home and tattle on me."

"You're right. I can't. After all, someone needs to before you get harmed."

"I'm not going to get injured. Can't we just drop this? And, Cole, please don't say anything to my parents, either."

Cole's expression turned wary. "Sorry I let the cat out of the bag. Though, if you don't mind me saying so, you should really be careful around that guy. Even Mr. Burns doesn't like him."

"He told you that?"

"*Jah.*"

"What has he been doing that's so bad?" Ben asked.

"Ignore him," Jenny said to Cole. "Don't worry about Shane. He's real nice. He's been a good friend."

"Really?"

Somehow Cole made that one word convey a whole mixture of emotions.

"*Really,*" responded Hannah. "Besides, this is my business. Don't you have other things to worry about?"

Hurt filled Cole's eyes. "I guess I do. Sorry I brought it up," he added before turning to walk away.

Remorse filled her as she realized just how rude and mean she was being. Cole was nice and kind. She was beginning to feel like she was two different people: one person who was the same as she had always been . . . and the other who was capable of being spiteful and vindictive.

What was wrong with her?

Ben's voice seared through her thoughts. "Jenny, what in the world have you been doing here in Hart County? Just how many secrets have you been keeping?"

Ignoring his questions, she glared at him. "Ben, you better not say anything about Shane to Mamm or Daed, *or* Hannah. Promise me you won't."

"I'm not going to make such a promise. You're obviously making a lot of bad decisions. Someone needs to talk some sense into you."

"Stop sounding so dramatic."

"It's not dramatic if I'm right."

Her parents would be so upset if they found out about the things she'd been doing. They'd be upset and hurt, too. Feeling panicked, she said, "If you tell anyone about me and Shane, I'll be sure to tell Mamm and Daed not to let you go to the Amish school. I'll tell them that you only want to go there because you hate Hannah."

Ben's eyes widened. "You know that ain't true."

"I do. But they don't."

"You're actually blackmailing me?"

"I'm not blackmailing you. It's a promise."

"I'm really starting to worry about you, Jenny," Ben said as he stood up.

"Where are you going?"

"Home, remember?" he muttered sarcastically. "Good luck getting home by yourself," he added as he started walking away. "And don't even think I'm going to cover for you. From now on, you are on your own."

As Jenny watched her brother walk away, she realized that he hadn't lied. She was now completely alone, and she had made it that way.

It didn't even matter that it was her own fault.

Chapter 11

Tuesday, July 19

It was late afternoon, and Jenny was once again nowhere to be found.

For some time, Hannah had debated whether or not to bother her parents with her worries about Jenny. She didn't want to worry them unnecessarily. She didn't want to give them even more stress, especially since her father seemed to be feeling so badly.

But it had become apparent that she had no choice.

They needed to be aware of how Jenny was acting. If they didn't, she could get hurt. After all, hadn't she arrived home late last night by herself? Someone needed to put a stop to Jenny's antics, and it was a foregone conclusion that it could not be Hannah.

"Mamm, Daed," she began as she walked into the living room, "I need to talk to you about something."

Her mother raised her head from the magazine she'd been leisurely thumbing through. "What is it, Hannah?" she asked in a weary voice.

That tone, together with her tired-looking posture, brought Hannah up short. Then, taking a closer look at her mother, she noticed that her eyes were red and the skin under her eyes looked bruised and puffy.

She wasn't sleeping.

Now she felt even worse about the news she was about to share. But though she hated to be the messenger of bad news, she also didn't know how to not say anything. She loved her sister, and because of that, she had to do this. Even if it was hard.

"I wanted to talk to you about Jenny." Sitting down on the ottoman in front of her father, she continued. "I don't know if you both have noticed, but she's been having some problems when it comes to telling the truth. She is also doing some strange things."

Just as she was about to list out Jenny's odd acts, including the whole issue with those daisies, her father tossed down the newspaper he'd been reading. "Aren't you a bit old to be tattling on your sister, Hannah?" he asked.

Stung, she stared at him in surprise. "I'm not

tattling. I'm trying to tell you that she's been doing some concerning things. I thought you'd want to know."

"She's a teenager," Mamm said. "She is going to make some mistakes. She is also going to be most interested in making friends. That means we need to give her some leeway."

"I suppose so, but this is different."

Her mother continued as if Hannah hadn't said a word. "She has also been helping around the house. A lot. She is a responsible young lady. There's no need for you to feel like you have to watch her every minute of the day."

"I'm not. But not only is she hanging around some people we don't know, she cut off the heads of all the daisies in the front yard."

Her mother stared at her blankly. "What in the world does that have to do with anything?"

Feeling like she was drowning in a pit, and not really sure what she was saying that her parents were finding fault with, Hannah got to her feet. "They were *daisies,* first of all. I'm not even sure how we got daisies in the yard. Are you?"

Her father shook his head.

"She said she didn't bring them to the house. But then she cut off the tops." Hannah stared at her parents, silently begging for them to understand how difficult this was for her.

Her mother sighed. "Hannah, we've been patient with your worries and have tried to help you get over your unnatural fear of everything. Now it's time that you tried to do that, too."

"Unnatural fear?" she echoed. "That's hardly fair. You know Trent's actions were scary. Even the police said so."

"That was months ago. And in another state," her father pointed out. "We've given you time and allowed you to stay cooped up inside this house for as long as you needed to. But this . . . this paranoia of yours? Well, it's got to stop."

She wasn't sure what she'd said that sounded paranoid. "Daed, you don't understand—"

"Those flowers were mine, Hannah," her mother said.

Hannah scanned her mother's face, attempting to understand everything that she was telling her. But it didn't make sense.

"Why would they be yours?" she asked, each word sounding as if it had been choked out of her. She felt like she was in a daze, in a dream. Anywhere but standing in front of her parents.

Mamm sighed. "My manager gave them to me after my first week at work. I left them outside because I wasn't sure where I could plant them without you being reminded of Trent," she explained, sounding very aggrieved. "That is why the flowers were outside, Hannah. It had nothing to do with your stalker."

"You were going to plant daisies in the yard?" Her voice sounded as incredulous as she felt.

116

"I can't believe you were going to do such a thing! I mean, you know how I feel about those flowers. You *know* how they make me feel."

"I realize that, but I couldn't very well refuse them. That's no way to behave at a new job."

Hannah supposed her mother couldn't have pushed them away. But wasn't there another way to handle receiving them? It seemed so very callous of her mother to bring them home. "You couldn't have simply given them to someone else?"

"You see? This is a good example of why you need to start thinking about other things besides your sister's comings and goings," her father said sternly. "Here, your mother has received a nice gift after a full week at a new, difficult job. A job that she had to take because we had to move."

"You said we also had to move because of your disease, Daed." Why were they being so insensitive?

"That is true, but we would have likely waited until Jenny finished her eighth-grade year. But you were doing so poorly, we had to take drastic measures."

"So Jenny's problems are my fault, too."

"We didn't say that," her mother said.

"It sure sounds that way, though. It sounds very much like that."

Standing up, she crossed the room and placed her hands on Hannah's shoulders. "Hannah, dear, please listen to me. We've turned this whole family upside down for you. We've all made sacrifices for your needs. But instead of you even thinking about your little sister, or how confused and lonely she must be feeling, you are only fixated on how those flowers remind you of your former boyfriend."

Hannah closed her eyes. Her mother's hands didn't feel warm or comforting. Instead, she felt trapped. She felt betrayed, too.

"Did you hear me, Hannah?" her mother asked. "Do you understand what I'm saying?"

Oh, yes, she heard. She would have never thought that her parents would be saying such things. It hurt. But she was also tired of arguing. Suddenly, all she wanted to do was escape to her room. Pulling from her mother's grip, she got to her feet.

Then she turned and looked her mother in the eye.

"I'm sorry about the flowers, Mother. You are exactly right. I guess I was only thinking about myself. I hadn't realized you all felt that way."

Her mother rubbed her temples. "Just, please, try to move on, Hannah. We need to be happy here."

And she wasn't letting them? "I'm trying. I mean, I will try. But will you talk to Jenny about her behavior?" Thinking quickly, she said, "Maybe she should find a job. Then she won't get into as much trouble."

"Are you listening to yourself, Hannah?" her mother asked, every word brimming with impatience. "You are making things up and seeing things in a skewed way. Jenny is not in trouble."

"Mamm, I am sure that she is seeing someone secretly. She's sneaking out . . . ."

"I don't think so. She is fine."

They weren't going to listen to her. Now feeling as worn-out as her mother looked after a full day of work, she said, "I'll go start on supper. I thought I'd make a cheeseburger casserole. Is that all right?"

"I don't care, dear," she said dismissively. "Anything is fine."

Without saying another word, Hannah turned to go to the kitchen. As she switched on burners and began browning the ground beef in order to put together the easy dish that they all used to enjoy at the big table in their old dining room, she looked out the window.

It had started to rain. It was just a light summer drizzle. Enough to soak anyone unlucky enough to get caught in it . . . but not enough to cause any big problems. As she continued to stare, she realized that the rain had created a slight fog to rise across the valley. It made it all look a little hazy. Almost dreamlike.

So much so, she could have sworn she saw a figure standing next to a pair of dogwoods in the distance.

A chill raced through her.

What if that was Trent? What if he found her and he was standing outside of her house again?

What if he was taking pictures of her again?

The edge of the laminate countertop cut into her palms as she gripped it hard and peered more closely out the window. Through the sheets of rain, she saw movement again. It had to be a man. A man lurking in the shadows of the woods beyond her.

A chill washed over her.

Needing someone else to see what she was seeing, she opened her mouth to call her parents, but stopped.

Her father said she was paranoid.

Her mother thought she was selfish and self-centered.

They both thought she was unable to move on from the past.

They loved her, but they were tired of her being so difficult.

She slumped. Maybe she was just making something out of nothing again. Maybe her mind was playing tricks on her.

Maybe her parents were right. She couldn't let the past go.

Deliberately, she turned back to the range. Moved the hamburger around on the frying pan. Tried very hard to pretend nothing was out of the ordinary.

But after less than a minute, she turned back around and stared out the window again. It was raining harder. Heavy drops splashed against the windowpanes. In the distance, lightning flashed, followed almost immediately by a clap of thunder.

Pressing one palm against the cold, condensation-lined window, Hannah continued to scan the area. Looking. Searching.

She didn't see a single thing.

When another bolt of lightning flashed, illuminating the woods for a brief instant, the area looked desolate again.

Almost bare.

Maybe she really was losing her mind. Maybe Trent's stalking had disturbed her so much that she now saw signs of him everywhere.

And if that was the case, she had no idea what she was going to do next.

Chapter 12

**Two days later
Thursday, July 21**

"You got a letter, Hannah!" Ben called out.

"*Danke*," Hannah murmured as she took it from him. Noticing that it had no return address, her hands shook as she tore open the envelope. When she realized it was from Kirsten, she breathed a sigh of relief.

Her brother raised his eyebrows. "You sure are excited to get a letter."

Not wanting him to know that she'd been afraid that the letter had come from Trent, she smiled weakly. "I guess I am. Like you, I miss my friends in Berlin."

The moment she said that, she waited for him to chide her. To blame her yet again for dislocating them all from everything they'd known.

But instead, he simply shrugged. "You know, I used to only think about all of my buddies there. But now I don't worry about them so much."

So glad that he didn't seem near as upset with her, she said, "That's *gut, jah*?"

"Yeah. I like Sam a lot, and I like his brother Isaac, too. None of them seem to mind that I've been spending a lot of time over at their house, either."

"I bet they are thinking that you're a good friend to have."

Ben rolled his eyes, but she could tell he was pleased by her compliment. Feeling more at ease than she had in days, she walked back to her room to read Kirsten's letter. She couldn't wait to once again be embroiled in Kirsten's love life and small concerns. Worrying about those things were so much easier than her parents, her sister, or that she was slowly losing her mind.

Once she'd closed the door, she opened the note and sat on her bed to read it carefully.

As she expected, the first paragraphs of the letter were all about her ongoing infatuation with Henry. Hannah smiled as Kirsten described in detail their latest argument, then in the next paragraph admitted that they'd kissed behind his barn when they were making up.

After that, she told Hannah she was sorry about how Jenny and Ben were making her so miserable, but reminded her that Jenny had always been a bit of a sourpuss.

Next, she updated Hannah on her family and the news on their friends. She filled her in on their girlfriends and who showed up for church.

Then she tackled Hannah's news about the daisies.

I have to admit that I feel the same way as you do about those plants, Hannah. Trent gave you at least six or seven bouquets of flowers, all of those white daisies. Of course you don't want to see them in your front yard. If I were you, I'd take them to the woods no matter what.

Trent was creepy!

Oh, I guess I should let you know that something weird happened to one of the first letters you wrote me. It was so sweet, I had put it in my planner, just so I could look at it when I was really missing you.

Just the other day, though, I realized that it was gone. I don't know what happened to it. I guess it fell out.

It's no big deal, but for some reason I thought I should tell you what happened. Just in case, you know, someone we know finds the letter and writes to you.

With another two paragraphs, Kirsten ended the letter.

Hannah read it twice more, trying unsuccessfully to pretend that she wasn't worried about Kirsten's story.

Surely, nothing could have happened to that letter. It would be ridiculous to imagine that the letter could have fallen out and somehow gotten into Trent's hands.

But if it did . . . then he now had her address.

He could have found her. Which might prove that she wasn't losing her mind after all.

Saturday, July 30

By the following Saturday, Hannah was starting to believe that she was going to only feel safe when she was away from her house.

Things at home had gotten worse. Her mother was working longer hours and her father seemed to be spending the majority of the day sitting in his easy chair in the living room.

He was often chilled, which meant he had taken to constantly burning logs in their fireplace. It made their small house smell like they were in the middle of a campfire as well as uncomfortably warm.

And while Ben was acting far more understanding and kind around her, he wasn't around as much. He'd taken a part-time job at a dairy farm nearby. He'd also convinced their parents to allow him to enroll in the local Amish school. Now he left the house at dawn and rarely returned before sunset.

Jenny was another story. She was only around to do her chores and sleep. Otherwise, she was gone, freely ignoring Hannah's attempts to control her or to help her with her studies. But her absence was better than her moody, restless disposition and sarcastic comments.

Though Hannah was a bit busier with the sandwich sale coming up, she now had far more free time than she'd had in years. She spent a lot of time wondering what to do with herself and dwelling on the past, even though she knew that wasn't healthy.

Each person in her family, in their own way, had abandoned her. She was now as alone as she'd ever been, only this time it wasn't by choice. Each morning, Hannah made breakfast, picked up around the house, and worked on laundry or other tasks that needed to be done. Then she either cared for her father or debated about whether to leave the house.

Some days were better than others. Some days, she was able to go through several hours without thinking about Trent or dwelling on the past. Other times, the shadows that she thought she saw would overpower her thoughts and she would be reduced to staying inside and staring out the window. Wishing things were different, but having no idea how to make them any different.

Her only bright spot had become Isaac. Like clockwork, he'd come by the house every afternoon. Together, they'd sit on her front porch or go on a short walk. She'd encourage him to talk to her about his siblings or his job.

And she would pretend she was far more normal than she actually was.

That morning, he'd picked her up and taken her to another meeting for the fund-raiser. When they'd arrived, everyone had gotten right to work.

Because of that, the meeting had quickly evolved into a fun get-together.

After visiting with the women for a while, Hannah had noticed a large hutch in the back of their hosts' yard. John and Karen happened to raise rabbits. After making sure that Karen didn't mind if she wandered out to see them, Hannah walked over.

The rabbits were big and super soft, and though

they lived in hutches, they seemed as happy to be around people as most house cats.

"Would you like to hold one?" one of Karen's younger sisters asked. "They like to be held."

"Sure."

"Here you go," the blond-haired girl said, handing her a pudgy dark-chocolate bunny. "This is Hershey."

Hannah held her close, enjoying the way her nose twitched as she looked at her curiously. "Aren't you sweet?" she murmured.

After smiling at her, the girl wandered off. Hannah sat down on the ground and petted the bunny.

Looking across the yard, she caught Maggie's eye. Maggie smiled at her but didn't approach.

Things really were going okay.

No one had looked at her like she was strange or asked her intrusive questions about her past or why she'd spent so much time alone when she'd first moved to Munfordville.

Instead, they seemed eager to get to know the person she was, without judgments.

Hannah was extremely grateful for that. Ever since Trent had left her that packet at the restaurant, Hannah had been doubting herself. Her family's impatience with her had exacerbated this. That, combined with the ever-present feeling that she was being watched, had made her wonder if everything that had happened was her fault.

Maybe she'd brought on Trent's actions somehow, though she'd had no idea what she'd done. Maybe she really was clinging to what had happened in some misguided attempt for attention. Why else would she have reacted to those daisies the way she had?

Why else would she have been so disturbed by Jenny cutting up the flowers and stems when no one else had been?

She was tired of revisiting her past and wishing things were different, especially since Isaac had seemed to consume her thoughts.

Walking to her side, Isaac was making no secret that he was amused by her fascination with the rabbit.

"I would have thought a sensible girl like you would have no patience for a chocolate-colored bunny, Hannah. But you can't seem to stop fussing with it." Looking like he was fighting off laughter, he said, "Don't tell me you didn't have rabbits up in Ohio, either."

"Lots of folks had rabbits, for sure. Just not me." Knowing he had a point, she laughed at herself. "Besides, I'm not actually fussing with her."

"No?"

"No. I'm cuddling her," she countered. "How could I not? She's so sweet."

He reached out and ran a finger down the rabbit's neck. "She is. Soft, too. Maybe you need one for yourself."

"Maybe, though raising a rabbit surely isn't a sensible undertaking. It's not like I could train it to do much."

He tilted his head to one side as he studied her. "I don't see what that matters. Sometimes a person just needs something because it makes him or her happy."

"That is true if one is a child."

"I think it's true at any age." He waited a beat, then continued, his voice turning lower. "I'm of the mind that you've been through enough hardship. If something makes you happy, you should reach for it."

"Even if it's chocolate bunnies?"

"*Jah.* Even if it's bunnies."

There had been something new in his voice. Something lilting and caring. Part of her wanted to reach out to him. She wanted to feel his rough, warm hand against hers. She wanted to reach out and hug him.

She was sure that his arms around her would comfort her in a way nothing else seemed to.

At the very least, it would alleviate the chill that seemed to have taken hold of her heart. To tell him all about her fears and share the worries she was experiencing. But what if he thought she was being ridiculous? What if he was so disturbed by her thoughts that he, too, pulled away from her?

Then she would be left even more alone. She

didn't think she could take that. No, she knew she couldn't.

"Hey."

"What?" Startled, Hannah glanced at him. When she saw he was staring at her curiously, she flushed. "Goodness. I'm sorry, I guess my mind drifted. I didn't mean to be rude."

"I didn't think you were being rude. I was worried about you. Are you okay? I thought I lost you there for a second."

"Maybe you did." She chuckled softly, hoping it didn't sound as forced as she felt it did. "I was just thinking about something that happened recently."

"Want to talk about it? I'm a good listener."

"*Nee.*"

He took a step back. "Okay . . ."

"I'm sorry." She attempted to smile in order to ease the tension that had risen between them. "It's just . . . well, what I was thinking wasn't very good. There are some things that have been going on at home that I can't seem to stop thinking about. It's certainly nothing for you to worry about."

"Are you worried about Jenny?" When she stared at him in surprise, he shrugged. "Sorry. I guess my family talks too much. Ben said something to Sam about your sister. Sam mentioned it last night when we were eating supper."

She was torn between being curious about what he'd heard and feeling disappointed that, in her own family, dinner discussions like that were a thing of the past.

Because Jenny was such a sore subject with her, and she didn't want to taint this sweet moment with him with more of her problems, she shook her head. "There's no need to apologize. I'm glad Ben is talking to Sam and that Sam is sharing things with you. But I wasn't thinking about my sister."

Seeing Maggie and some other women laughing as they were writing notes on notecards, Hannah got to her feet. "I think I'm going to go to see if those girls need any help."

Turning to where she was looking, he grinned. "It looks like they certainly might. Do you still want to walk back home together?"

"I do."

"I'll come get you in about an hour."

"*Danke*, Isaac." She hoped he knew she was thanking him for more than just walking her home.

It was for everything. For not pressing her about all of her secrets. For easily accepting her flaws. It was also for giving her space while at the same time promising her that he was not going to leave her.

"I'm happy to walk with you anytime, Hannah," he said softly.

She smiled at him again before walking over to the girls.

"Hannah!" Maggie cried out exuberantly. "Please

tell me that you know how to make heads or tails of all these lists and people."

"I might. I'm actually pretty good at organizing things."

Karen looped her hand around Hannah's elbow. "Girls, she's ours to keep."

When Hannah laughed at Karen's exuberant claim, Maggie smiled at her with true warmth. "She's right, you know. You're stuck with us, Hannah Hilty. We might never let you go."

"*Gut!*" She laughed again, truly enjoying the silly comments.

But the truth was that she didn't want to leave their company. Here she felt accepted, loved. Safe.

Chapter 13

Saturday, July 30

"Do you really think we're going to be able to sell almost a thousand sandwiches?" Hannah asked Isaac as they walked down the road, back toward their houses.

Looking over at her, Isaac thought she looked cute. For once, she looked completely relaxed walking by his side. Almost as if he was the one person she could be herself with.

He liked that. He was also very glad that she'd forgiven him for his callous first impression.

And that their relationship was progressing forward. Every time they were together, Hannah seemed to joke and laugh a little bit more. She met his gaze more often. Smiled softly at him. They were becoming closer. Becoming a couple.

He had no idea where their relationship was headed. Maybe they would one day get married. Maybe they were destined to be just friends. Only the Lord knew that. How He wanted it to go, Isaac didn't know. But it didn't really matter, as long as he had Hannah's friendship.

"I don't know," he replied. "A thousand is an awful lot of sandwiches. To be honest, I was thinking five hundred was a good number. But Maggie and Paul are hopeful and think it can be done. They make a good argument for trying, I think. Every bit will go toward a good cause."

Her eyes widened. "If we charge ten dollars for each sandwich meal, that's going to be ten thousand dollars!"

"I know. That's a lot of money. Plus, sometimes folks even give a little bit more, since it's for such a good cause. I have no idea how high their bills are, but I'm hopeful that our sale will put a sizable dent in their hospital bills."

"I hope so." Her voice turned soft. "I feel so badly for them. I would imagine that it's hard enough to care for a new baby without wondering how they are going to pay for a surgery."

Isaac thought her worried expression was

sweet. Giving into temptation, he wrapped his arm around her shoulders, and gave her a little hug. When she looked up at him, he smiled encouragingly. "It's a good thing we're doing, Hannah. It's good for them, and it's good for all of us, too. I, for one, am guilty of worrying so much about my own problems that I forget that many people have far greater problems on their plates."

"Amen to that."

"Now all we have to hope is that you are an early riser. Are you?"

"Of course I am."

"You said that awfully quickly," he teased. "So quickly, I'm wondering if I should believe you."

"That's smart of you." Looking embarrassed, she said, "You found out my secret. Even though most Amish girls are supposed to like to rise with the sun, that ain't me."

"It's not, hmm?"

"Not at all. Oh, I'll get up, but I'm never too easy about it. It's a lengthy process."

"I'm just the opposite. I wake up with the sun, ready for the day."

She rolled her eyes. "Show off."

"What do you need in order to get you going?" he asked, liking their easy, irreverent conversation. "Lots of coffee or a full breakfast? A rooster calling?"

"Just a cup of *kaffi*."

He couldn't resist teasing her some more. "Just one?"

"All right. It's more like two or three cups."She shrugged. "I don't know why I need that caffeine, but I do."

"I'll arrive at your house on Saturday with a coffee cup from Calvin's. It will give me an excuse to stop in and get a couple of sausage biscuits." Calvin's was his favorite coffee shop.

"You don't have to do that," she said around a giggle. "I promise, I'll have had plenty of coffee before you arrive. I'll be ready with bells on."

"I don't mind. It's the least I can do after roping you into this project. Especially since we'll need to leave at five in the morning."

"Leave at five? Oh, brother. In that case, yes, please bring me some of your Calvin *kaffi*, Isaac Troyer. And maybe one of those sausage biscuits, too."

She sounded so aggrieved, he burst out into laughter. "It's so kind of you to give in to my offer so gracefully."

Her cheeks flushed. "You really don't mind, do you?"

"Of course not. I'm just teasing ya." He was about to tease her some more, just to hear her giggle and watch her eyes light up with mischief, when he saw movement in the woods next to them. It looked like a man wearing a white shirt

135

and denims. A man who had been keeping pace with them.

Curious, he stopped and craned his head, hoping to catch sight of whatever he saw again.

Hannah turned around when she realized he wasn't still by her side. "Isaac? What's wrong?"

"Nothing. I . . . well, I could have sworn I saw someone just on the other side of that line of trees."

"No one could be there." Stepping closer to him, a new thread of doubt entered her tone. "Could they?"

"Well, sure. Someone could be on the path." When she looked confused, he added, "That's where the old walking path is. The one that you were walking on the first day we met. Remember? It's filled with rosebushes, poison ivy, and oak. No one walks there who knows better."

She shivered. "I sure learned my lesson. I didn't get poison ivy, but I got a good amount of scratches and scrapes on my arms. And a slew of prickers on my shoelaces."

"That's why no one ever goes over there unless it's in the middle of winter."

He kept his eyes glued to the woods, looking for any discrepancy or any trace of color that shouldn't be there. No luck, though. Maybe it had been his imagination.

Beside him, Hannah was looking even more agitated. "I bet it was just somebody taking a shortcut."

"I bet you're right," he murmured, though he knew what he saw. He knew the woods and surrounding areas well. He'd also had a lifetime of hunting in his back pocket. He was used to looking for the slightest slip of movement.

Scanning the woods again, he let his gaze relax. He hoped that would allow him to see the whole area better, as well as being able to spot the white fabric sticking out like a sore thumb.

"Can we go, Isaac?"

Surprised by how panicked she sounded, he stared at her more closely. Hannah had a faint coating of perspiration on her forehead and upper lip. She was frightened.

"Of course," he said, wrapping an arm around her shoulders again as he guided her forward.

This time he let it stay while they walked. She was shaking and scared. When she leaned closer to him, he felt like he'd accomplished something important.

She was trusting him now.

"It's going to be all right," he soothed. "I bet it was nothing. I'm sorry if I scared you."

"You didn't scare me," she began before shaking her head impatiently. "I mean, yes, that did scare me, but it wasn't your fault. If you saw someone, I'm glad you told me. I don't ever want to be kept in the dark about things like this."

That comment concerned him. "Were you kept in the dark before? Did someone know about this man's interest in you and not tell you?"

"*Nee*. At least, I don't think so. I guess it was just a feeling I had." Pulling away from his embrace, she looked into his eyes. "I was blind-sided, Isaac. That's the only way I can describe it. I went from talking to Trent, to seeing him a couple of times, to telling him that I was sure things between us wouldn't work out. I thought he agreed."

"But he didn't."

"*Nee*." Staring forward now, she added, "And that was what was so strange. He seemed to agree with me. Once I told him that I had made up my mind, I was going to join the church and be baptized so I couldn't continue seeing him, I hardly saw him."

"But then you did?"

She nodded. "Every once in a while, he would show up at the restaurant with daisies for me. Once he was at the library when I was there."

"Did he approach you then?"

"*Nee*. He just stared at me, which made me feel embarrassed. But then, weeks after that, the notes started."

Isaac was flabbergasted. "I'd assumed this man's infatuation only lasted a couple of weeks."

"*Nee*, it was longer than that. Much longer. I hung around him when I was eighteen. We only dated—if you could even call it that—for a couple of weeks. It wasn't anything serious. It wasn't until several months later that he gave me the first batch of daisies."

"And now you are twenty." She'd been dealing with this man's unwanted advances for almost two years.

"*Jah*. Now I am twenty. I really wish I could go back and tell my younger self to be far more circumspect. It would have saved me a lot of pain."

"I think all of us wish we could do that. Everyone makes poor choices. But what is happening to you ain't your fault. You are not to blame."

Her eyes widened.

"You're right. Thank you for reminding me of that."

"No problem." Smiling, he said, "You know what? We're turning into a mighty *gut* pair."

She tucked her head, but not quickly enough to hide her smile. "Indeed."

He knew he'd keep those words and that smile close to his heart for days.

Chapter 14

Wednesday, August 3

Their parents were gone for the day. They'd kept their destination a secret, but Hannah hoped that they were going to see the doctor again. Her father looked weaker and her mother looked more stressed as each day passed.

As usual, Hannah was home. She was cooking supper and supposedly keeping tabs on Jenny. *Supposedly* was the key word, because Jenny was acting particularly sullen. That was probably because she had gotten in trouble for ignoring most of her chores. When Daed had found out, he'd grounded her for the week.

But while Jenny was the one who had disobeyed her parents, Hannah was feeling that she was the one being punished. Jenny couldn't be more difficult if she tried.

Looking over her shoulder at her sister yet again, she said, "Jenny, if you don't want to help me make bread or cookies for the sandwich sale, you are going to have to do your studies."

"I'm too old for the assignments you gave me."

"If it's that easy for ya, then you should have no problem finishing it quickly. Ain't so?" She took care to keep her voice light, because if there was one thing she actually did know, it was that Jenny was not finding the work too easy.

In fact, she was having such a hard time, she was putting it off as long as she could.

Jenny glared at her. "You have no idea what you're talking about."

"I think I do. I did much of that same work when I was fourteen."

"Well, *Shane* says no one needs to know anything about national parks." She tossed her head. "Especially Amish girls."

"You know that's not true. We're American. Most Americans know quite a bit about Yosemite and Yellowstone and the Grand Canyon."

"It ain't like I'm ever going to see such things."

"Of course you might. We know lots of Amish who go on bus vacations. Why, Kirsten and I had always planned to go on a trip."

"Where to?"

"Pinecraft."

Jenny picked up her pencil and started to doodle on the top of the page. "But you don't want to go any longer?"

Hannah paused before answering. She'd heard something new in her sister's voice. Something that sounded a lot like hope in the middle of all that bitterness. "What is this really about? Are you wishing you were traveling now or something?"

"What's wrong with me can't be solved by going on a bus trip, Hannah."

"What will solve it?"

"Leaving here. Doing something different. Being someone different."

"Jenny, just talk to me."

"That's what we've been doing."

"*Nee*, I mean, talk to me. *Really* talk to me. What is upsetting you so much? I know you miss your friends back in Berlin, but I'm starting to get the feeling that missing your friends ain't at the heart of what's really going on." Wondering who this Shane person was, she asked, "Does it have to do with *Shane*?"

Jenny swallowed. "*Nee*. I mean, not really."

Feeling like her sister had finally given her a small opening, she said, "Who *is* Shane?"

"No one you know."

"Oh? Why is that?"

"Because you don't," Jenny snapped.

Oh, but Jenny could be trying! Needing a moment, Hannah picked up the knife and carefully started slicing a carrot. "You may not believe me, but I really do just want to help you. What is wrong?"

For a long moment, Hannah wondered if her sister was going to answer her at all.

Hannah next picked up an onion and started slicing it, hoping that the break would compel Jenny to finally speak to her honestly.

"I feel so stuck," Jenny blurted, her eyes suddenly filling with tears. "Everything is different, but it's also just the same. The same as it ever was."

"Because we're Amish?" When Jenny looked ready to bolt, Hannah turned away from the cutting board and walked to her side.

"It's . . . it's the fact that we moved. That we are living in this little house. That Daed is sick and you are afraid of everyone and everything. It's that Mamm is working long hours and looking tired."

Hannah knew all these things. She also knew that any one of those items could bother anyone, most especially a fourteen-year-old girl.

However, Hannah was pretty sure that wasn't everything.

That was why she sat down in the chair next to Jenny and clasped her hand. Silently conveying that she wasn't alone. Not by a long shot.

The tension between them grew, slowly became even more strained. Jenny looked like she was not only ready to tell Hannah everything but also that she was scared to utter a word.

Another minute passed.

Jenny opened her mouth. Shut it. At last, she blurted, "I think what happened to you is my fault."

Nothing could have been more surprising. Biting back an instant response, Hannah took her time to form her words, trying her best to keep them easy and calm. "Why would you say that?"

Jenny licked her bottom lip. Swallowed. Inhaled. "Trent used to write me little notes after you broke things off with him."

Anger and hurt rushed through Hannah. "I don't understand," she bit out, trying her best to keep from jumping to her feet and yelling. "You're telling me that you saw Trent privately?"

"*Nee*! I've never met him."

"Then I don't understand. Please, explain yourself. *Now*." She let go of Jenny's hand and folded her arms across her chest in a small attempt to prepare herself with the realization that Jenny had likely betrayed her.

Jenny took a breath, then mumbled, "A couple of months after you broke up with him, I found a note in my backpack." Blushing now, she said, "It was just a little note. Saying that he had heard a lot about me and was sad that we had never met in person." After a pause, she added, "He asked if we could become pen pals."

"What did you do?"

"I wrote him back and said yes."

"Jenny, how could you?"

Jenny winced. "I know what it sounds like, but it wasn't like that. I was twelve back then. He seemed nice. We had a secret spot to leave each other notes. It was fun."

Hannah could hardly wrap her head around what she was hearing. "So all the while he was tormenting me, you were being his secret friend?"

"*Nee*."

"It sure sounds that way."

"It wasn't. All we did was write each other little

notes once or twice a month. I'd tell him about my day and he would act like he cared."

"Oh, Jenny." Hannah ached to yell at her. To tell her that she couldn't believe anyone could be so naïve, but that would be the pot calling the kettle black. At first, she'd been caught up in Trent's attention, too.

And what better way than to encourage a young girl than to write secret notes?

Tears were running down Jenny's cheeks now. "Please don't hate me. I didn't know he was bad. I just thought you didn't like him anymore. I felt sorry for him."

"He used you. He took advantage of you."

"I . . . I was flattered by his attentions." Gazing at Hannah, she said, "You are so pretty, Hannah. Everyone says so. And smart. My teacher used to ask me why I wasn't smart like you."

"You are smart."

"Not like you." Grabbing a napkin from the holder in the center of the table, she blew her nose. Then blurted, "You are so good, too. You always do what's expected of you."

"Not hardly."

"You used to. That is why I wrote to him for so long. But I promise, when he started doing mean things to you, I stopped."

"Did he get mad at you?"

Jenny shrugged. "I don't know. I just stopped going to the spot where we traded letters."

Releasing a ragged sigh, Jenny continued. "Then Trent sent those photographs to you. I guess he sent them to you because I wasn't nice to him anymore."

"None of this was your fault. He would have done those things to me even if you hadn't written him notes," Hannah said. "He used you, and I'm very sorry for that."

"I'm sorry, too." Jenny blinked rapidly, obviously trying hard to stop crying.

Hannah felt for her, but knew she had to be honest. "I wish you would have told me about this months ago."

"I was too ashamed." Closing her eyes, she added, "Plus, I knew you'd be mad at me."

Hannah knew Jenny needed some reassurance. She needed it like she needed to breathe. And because, very recently, she'd ached for some reassurances of her own but had instead felt forgotten, Hannah gave her sister what she needed, even though she was hurting. "Trent was wily. He used his looks and flattery and what-ever else he could think of to manipulate me. It's obvious he did that to you, too."

Jenny relaxed slightly. "He made me feel good —even when I knew deep inside that what he told me were lies."

"I'm so sorry."

Jenny sniffed. "I know. It makes no sense, right? I mean, you are so pretty. Much prettier than me.

Everyone has always said that. Why would I think that he would ever think that I was special, too?"

"First, you *are* special. You know that I'm not prettier than you. Looks don't matter much, anyway."

Jenny scoffed. "Of course they do. Look at me. I'm all arms and legs. You were never like that."

"Sure I was." Choosing each of her words with care, she said, "Jenny, I am six years older than you. When you are twenty, I'm sure you'll look much like me, but even better, because you'll look like you." She smiled, but she feared her words sounded as brittle as she felt inside. Was Trent's pursuit of her compounded by Jenny's jealousy?

And had Jenny ignored all that their parents had taught her? Did she really think one's looks mattered so much? Had she become that vain?

"Sometimes, Trent would ask me about you," Jenny blurted as if she needed to finally purge all of her secrets. "He'd ask me about your schedule. About what you did. If you were seeing anyone new."

All of it was hard to hear, but Hannah did her best to be nonjudgmental and listen.

"What did you say?"

Looking even more ravaged, Jenny said, "I told him. I used to tell him all about you."

"But I didn't do anything. I worked and went to the library, and did things with Kirsten. I helped out at home."

"I told him that. At first."

Foreboding filled her. "But then?"

"But then that wasn't good enough. So I made something up. I told him you'd found a new boyfriend who you were seeing secretly. That really made him mad."

Everything inside of her was screaming for her to tell Jenny to stop. To stop talking. To stop saying such things. But she needed to hear the whole story. It had stopped being about Jenny and about her again. She needed to understand. "What, exactly, did you tell him, sister?"

"I told him that the man you were seeing was a customer. That you were in love."

"I canna believe you did such a thing."

"That was why Trent started taking pictures of you, so he could catch you with this man. He would ask me to leave daisies at places where you were going to be."

"That is how they got there. It was because of you. Not him?"

Looking thoroughly miserable, she nodded.

Remembering something else, Hannah asked, "Did you bring those daisies to Mamm? Does she think they're from work but they're really from you?"

"Definitely not! They were as much of a shock to me as they were to you."

Hannah stared at her hard. "Are you telling the truth or lying?"

"I'm telling the truth. That's why I cut them up. Because seeing them scared me, too. When I saw them, I thought it meant that he was here."

"Have you stayed in contact with him? Does he know where we are?"

"*Nee.*"

"When did you stop talking to him?"

"I stopped right before he sent you that packet. When he didn't see you with another man, he got angry with me. He said he didn't need me anymore. And that's when I realized that he'd never liked me in the first place. He had just been pretending to be nice so I would give him information about you." Tears were now falling down her face, dropping unchecked onto her chest and lap and the table, too. "He'd never thought of me as anything but a way to get to you."

"He is evil, Jenny. He used me when I was wanting to be flattered by his attentions. Then he used you when he wanted something he couldn't have. What he did wasn't your fault."

"Are you ever going to be able to forgive me?"

Hannah blinked. She noticed then that Jenny was holding her hand tightly, almost as if she was afraid that Hannah was going to let it go.

Placing her other palm on Jenny's hand, so her hand was cradled in both of hers, she spoke from the heart. "Of course, I will forgive you."

"Really? I wouldn't."

"Am I hurt? Yes, I am. Do I wish you hadn't

kept such a big secret from me and Mamm and Daed, and Ben, too? Yes, I do. I wish you would have told us."

"They would have hated me."

"They would have been disappointed, but they wouldn't have hated you. Actually, I think they would have felt relief. Now so much of what happened back in Berlin makes sense."

"I'm so sorry, Hannah."

Hannah hadn't realized it, but that was what she'd needed to hear. She could forgive anything if there was true remorse, and there was. Jenny was obviously remorseful about what she'd done.

"Is there anything else that's made you so upset and worried?" She raised an eyebrow. "Another terrible secret you wish to unload? If so, now would be a *gut* time to share it."

Jenny smiled. "*Nee.*" Her eyes widened and she slapped a hand over her mouth. "I can't believe I'm smiling right now."

"Don't even think of apologizing for that." Realizing how much better seeing her sister's happiness made her feel, she said, "Your smile feels like a rainbow. Something pretty to look at after a terrible storm." She smiled back at Jenny, feeling lighter than she had in weeks.

Of course they were going to have to revisit everything Jenny had done, but for now, it felt like Jenny was finally coming back to her, and Hannah was grateful for that.

Standing up, she held out her hands. "Give me a hug. Then we'll work on supper."

Jenny's chair scraped back as she surged to her feet and launched herself into Hannah's arms. "I really am sorry. And I love you, Hannah."

"I love you, too. No matter what happens, I will always love you." After giving her a little squeeze, she pulled away. "Now. Let's put away these books, wash our faces, and work on supper."

Jenny had just turned to pick up the textbooks when the door was flung open and Ben, Sam, and Isaac walked in.

All three of them looked tense and worried.

Hannah turned to them. "What happened?"

"Maybe you should sit down, Hannah," Isaac said.

She saw something in Isaac's eyes that gave her chills. "Is it about our parents?" Grasping at straws, she blurted, "Is my father worse?"

"It ain't about Daed," Ben blurted out, breaking her connection with Isaac.

"What is it about, then?"

He inhaled deeply, making her wonder if he was having trouble catching his breath from running or because he was so scared or upset.

"Ben!" Jenny said. "What is wrong?"

To their surprise, it was Sam who addressed their confusion. He held up a trio of daisies, encased in a single sheet of red tissue paper and secured with a black satin ribbon.

151

"We thought we saw him," Ben blurted. "Sam and I were walking on that path in the woods and there was a man up ahead of us. He looked just the way you described Trent. When I called out to him, he ran."

"Where did you get the flowers?"

"They were on your doorstep," Isaac said, his expression serious.

"That's not all, though, Hannah," Ben said quietly.

He held out a manila envelope. "We think he left you this, too."

Showing that her worst fear had become a reality. Trent had returned to taunt her again.

She closed her eyes. "Oh, my heavens. He's done it again. He's taken my picture."

Chapter 15

Wednesday, August 3

Every protective instinct that Isaac possessed kicked into gear when he saw how petrified Hannah was. He took charge of the situation, even though she hadn't asked for his help.

"You don't know that this is from Trent," Isaac said as he snatched the envelope from Ben's hand. After tossing it on the counter, he reached for Hannah's hands. "But what really matters is that you don't need to do a single thing," he soothed.

"I do, though. It's right here. I can't pretend it didn't arrive."

"That's true. However, we can ignore everything inside of this envelope. We can simply throw it away." Liking this idea, he softened his tone. "Hannah, you don't have to give him the satisfaction of reading his words. We certainly don't need you being frightened." Hating the new look of trepidation in her eyes, he added recklessly, "I'll make sure you are okay."

"You don't understand how it is, Isaac," she said in a weary tone of voice. "It isn't a matter of me buying into Trent's anger or even of becoming frightened by his photos. While he feeds on my fears, I don't think that's his only motivation. This . . . this correspondence"—she pointed to the sealed envelope—"it's a deliberate action. Almost like it has become a game for him."

"If it's a game, you don't have to play."

"That would be true, if he were a rational sort. But Trent ain't." With new emphasis in her voice, she said, "Isaac, he is not going to stop."

He hated how defeated she sounded.

Maybe, back when she was in Berlin, she had good reason. But he was at her side now. Surely, she realized, she didn't have to face these mind games on her own any longer? "You don't know that for certain."

"I'm afraid I do." She turned her head. Looked

down at her lap and played with the folds of her apron.

Isaac didn't know if she didn't want to look at him or if she was retreating into herself again.

To his surprise her sister, Jenny, approached Hannah from behind and wrapped her arms around her waist. Effectively offering her comfort without stifling her.

After a brief hesitation, Hannah released Isaac's hand and covered Jenny's hands with her own. He watched her pinched expression ease.

Jenny turned to Isaac. "I agree with my sister. This is how Trent's stalking all started. First, Trent would offer Hannah small bouquets of flowers."

"Daisies," Ben added. Shaking his head, he said, "There were so many. So many white daisies. I don't know where he got all of them."

"Then he started writing her notes," Jenny said.

"Which she never answered."

While Hannah remained silent, Jenny continued their tale. "Then he started sending Hannah pictures of herself. Some would be innocent-looking, like of Hannah walking on the street. A public place where anyone could have taken it."

"It was creepy, but we figured it was impossible to monitor, on account of people taking snapshots on their phones all the time," Ben explained.

"But then he started taking pictures of my sister when she was completely alone."

"I never saw him, though I always thought I was being watched," Hannah admitted in a voice that didn't quite hide her tremors. "It was a terrible sensation. I never felt like I was completely alone."

"All of us began to feel that way," Jenny admitted.

Hannah continued. "I began to fear for my family and my friends. No one wants to be constantly worried about being photographed."

Hannah's story was painful for him to hear. He hated that she was still so affected by the memories. But far more upsetting was the fact that this wasn't in her past, it was all happening again.

"Hannah, I see how hard this is. You don't need to talk about it."

Isaac didn't want Hannah to have to revisit Trent's stalking all over again. He wanted to help her. He ached to help her. No one should ever look like she did. Forlorn and without hope.

Looking at him, she simply shrugged. "It doesn't matter if I want to talk about it or not. It happened and it's happening again. Running away didn't help."

Picking up the envelope, Isaac turned to Ben and Jenny. "I'm confused by how much he ignored the police's warnings. When was the first time your father contacted the police?"

Ben tilted his head as he tried to remember. "I canna remember exactly. What do you think,

Jenny? Did Daed go talk to the sheriff after the fourth or the fifth envelope?"

"Daed waited longer than that. I think it was more like after the seventh or eighth."

"Daed finally went down to the sheriff's office the morning I started crying about it at breakfast," Hannah said.

Isaac was horrified. "Your father waited that long?"

Jenny answered. "Mamm and Daed didn't want to get the English involved."

Isaac could only imagine how Hannah had been living. No doubt, she had been living in fear, or at least with a degree of wariness. Always wondering when she was going to receive another bouquet or another envelope. It also was becoming obvious that she hadn't gotten all that much support, either. She probably had to brace herself to hear her father's brush-off.

It made him angry that she'd gone through such a nightmare, essentially alone. Even though it sounded like her siblings weren't as distant from her as he'd originally thought, they were also too young to lean on in an instance like that. "That was a mistake," he bit out. "Your father should have put a stop to this right away."

"He's said that he wished he had," Ben said quietly. "I think we all have regrets on how we handled it."

"I should have been more open about it,"

Hannah said. "A lot of times, I wouldn't tell anyone about the flowers or notes I received. I just kept it to myself. Kept it secret."

"Who can blame you?" Isaac murmured. "Forgive me, but it sounds like your parents wanted to pretend nothing was happening."

Hannah shared a look with Ben and Jenny, who had released her embrace and was now standing across from Isaac with her arms folded over her chest. "Now we realize they had other things on their mind," Hannah said.

"Dad is going to be upset that this has now followed Hannah," Jenny supplied.

Hannah lifted her chin. "I don't think any of us took Trent's infatuation with me seriously at first. It wasn't their fault."

"I'm not trying to be critical, Hannah, but I think you should handle things differently this time around." Before she could interrupt, Isaac added, "Actually, I think we should go to the sheriff right now. Give him this bouquet and let him open the envelope."

Twin spots of color flared in Hannah's cheeks. "Don't you think we should see what is inside the envelope first? It might be nothing."

"It already is something. It doesn't matter if there is a note inside that says he's sorry or if there is a photo of you just sitting on your front stoop. If he is still contacting you, it is something."

"I don't know. Going to the sheriff is a big step.

Plus, my problems are new to them. They won't understand why I'm so upset."

"I'm pretty sure I saw him, sister," Ben said. "He's being bold because he doesn't think you're going to fight back."

"Perhaps." She still looked unsure.

"Ben is right," Sam supplied. "That's what bullies do, *jah*? They push and push and hurt until someone fights back."

Jenny nodded. Looking far older than her years, she said, "The boys are right, Hannah. It's time to get the authorities involved."

Hannah still looked torn. "But what if Mamm and Daed say I shouldn't go to the sheriff?"

"I think we should go right now, before they return," Isaac said. He didn't want to go against her parents' wishes, but he felt very strongly—if they waited, nothing good was going to happen.

"They are going to be upset if I do that."

"Haven't you heard that it's always easier to beg for forgiveness than ask permission? Let's go and deal with their reaction when we get back."

"You sound so sure that this is the right thing to do."

"I am," assured Isaac. At the least, he considered, Hannah would be even more frightened. And at the worst?—this Trent would become even bolder. Maybe this time, he wouldn't stop at simply taking pictures of Hannah. Maybe this time, he'd want to talk to her. Or something worse.

Isaac didn't want to distress her, but he also wanted to make his point. "If he's followed you here, he's serious, Hannah. He's not going to stop with just delivering photos of you."

Hannah lifted her eyes to meet his gaze. In their depths, he saw confusion and pain . . . and, perhaps, appreciation? The myriad of emotions made her eyes look like they were a dozen other colors. If he and Hannah had been alone, he would have enfolded her in his arms and held her securely—to make sure she realized he wasn't going to leave her alone, not until she wanted him to leave.

He was actually thinking he might do that now. He didn't really care who he shocked. She needed to know that someone was on her side. But before he could either give her a hug or offer more reassurances, Jenny spoke again.

"You don't have to worry, Hannah. This time, you won't be alone. I'll go to the sheriff with you."

"Me, too," said Ben. "And don't say I'm too young. I'm not."

The corners of her lips turned up. "I wasn't going to say that. You are being very tough. Tougher than me."

"I'm going, too," Isaac said. "And I'm going to stay by your side when you talk to your parents."

"You'd do that?"

"Hannah, I'm going to stay by your side for as long as you need me to. For as long as you want me to." Staring at her, he lowered his voice. "I never want you to ever think you have to face anything alone again."

"I'm going to go, too," Sam blurted.

Ben turned to him. "You? Why?"

Sam shrugged. "Because I count. And I'm here." He lifted his chin. "And I care, too."

Hannah looked around the room, her gaze at last landing on the offending envelope. "You all are too much," she said with a low laugh. "You make me feel overwhelmed with gratitude. I don't know what to say."

"How about you say that we're all going to go to the sheriff's office right now?" Isaac said.

"We have to do this now, don't we?"

Ben picked up the envelope. "Go grab me a tote, Jenny."

Opening a closet, Jenny got out a small canvas bag. When she handed it to her brother, he put both the envelope and the bouquet of daisies in it.

"Let's go," Ben said. "It's time."

It was time. Time for Hannah to stop worrying and looking over her shoulder. Time for this Trent to be stopped.

Because Isaac knew one thing without a doubt —Hannah needed Trent's stalking of her to end. Only then would she be able to move forward.

Only then, Isaac felt, would she be able to think of him the way he was already thinking about her.

As the person in his life he'd been waiting for.

Chapter 16

Wednesday, August 3

Sheriff Brewer was in his mid-forties, was prematurely balding, looked like he enjoyed running, and had a whisper of fine lines around his gray eyes.

He also had a way of staring at a person that made one think that no one else was in the room.

It was disconcerting. Disconcerting enough to make Hannah very glad that she wasn't by herself. Instead, she was very far from being alone. She was surrounded by both of her siblings and Isaac and Sam Troyer.

They were all standing around in the sheriff's office, which was actually a trailer in the back of the courthouse. There was some construction nearby and a sign that thanked the taxpayers for the new offices and jail.

Though Hannah figured the sheriff, his deputies, and the office staff were going to enjoy their new place of work, she was mighty glad they were in the somewhat shabby trailer. It made her feel like Sheriff Brewer was more approachable and less intimidating—and she needed to feel that in a bad way.

"Are you sure none of y'all want to take a seat?"

he asked, looking slightly amused by Hannah's group. "We could probably round up some more metal chairs for you."

"I'm fine with standing," Isaac said.

"Me, too," said Ben and Sam almost at the same time.

"I'm not going to sit down if Hannah doesn't," Jenny said.

"And I'm too nervous to sit," Hannah admitted, rounding out their round of explanations.

"All right, then." Looking down at his notes, he said, "So from what I understand, you had a stalker by the name of Trent Ritchie back in Ohio, you moved to escape him, and you have reason to believe he has decided to follow you here to Hart County."

"*Jah*. That is correct," Hannah said.

Opening the canvas tote they'd brought with them, he continued. "He also sent you a bouquet of daisies."

"Yes. That was on my doorstep."

He held up the envelope. "Along with this?"

Hannah felt her pulse race as she stared at the envelope. "Yes."

Sheriff Brewer walked around his desk and sat down behind it. "Tell me again why you decided not to open it?"

"I was afraid to see what picture he took of me," Hannah said.

Isaac stepped closer to her. "I also told her that

maybe we should wait because there might be fingerprints on the photo."

"That was good thinking," Sheriff Brewer murmured. "If, of course, there actually is a photograph in here from this man."

He didn't believe her. He thought she was making more of an issue about this than he thought was reasonable.

Maybe he even thought she was wasting his time?

Nerves got ahold of her again. Unable to stop herself, Hannah twisted her fingers together, practically pinching the skin around the tips.

"Don't do that," Isaac whispered into her ear. "This was the right thing to do."

She exhaled. "I hope so."

Sheriff Brewer stared at her steadily. "Your boyfriend there is right, Miss Hilty. Coming to see us was, indeed, the right thing to do."

Her breath caught at the sheriff's mistaken impression of them. Warily, she glanced at Isaac.

But as if he could read her mind, he only smiled. Right then and there, she realized it didn't really matter what the sheriff thought of their relationship. She and Isaac were something. Maybe not boyfriend and girlfriend, but there was something significant between them.

Returning her thoughts back to the envelope, she said, "I just don't want to be making something out of nothing."

"Let's not worry about that." Sheriff Brewer opened a drawer, pulled out some white latex gloves, and a letter opener. "How about we go ahead and see what's inside, all right?"

Hannah nodded.

He paused. "Do you want anyone to leave?" Looking a little chagrined, he said, "In case it's a . . . well, a compromising photo?"

The tension in the room rose.

Hannah wondered if it was because they feared, after escorting her here that she'd make them leave; or that they were just now realizing they could be seeing something embarrassing or invasive. Her heart started pounding as she imagined how awful it would feel if everyone saw a photo of her partially undressed.

But she couldn't imagine how that would have ever happened.

Hannah didn't know how Trent could have taken a compromising picture. After all, she'd hardly left the house until the last two weeks.

But then, as she looked around the room, she realized that she needed their support. These people weren't going to think worse of her no matter what they saw. Instead, they were going to be upset on her account.

"Maybe you could look at it first?" she asked. "Unless it's very embarrassing, I think I'm going to want everyone to remain here."

Without another word, Sheriff Brewer neatly

sliced through the seal of the envelope, peeked in, then pulled out what looked like a note and several photographs.

Hannah gripped Isaac's arm as the sheriff read the note, then glanced at the photos.

Sheriff Brewer's face was carefully blank as he looked at the third and last photo, then scanned the note again. At last, he placed the note and the three photos back into the envelope.

His expression was far more subdued and tense than it had been. He cleared his throat.

"Hannah, it seems your concerns were justified. These photos are fairly disturbing."

Chill bumps appeared on her arms. "Are they from Trent?"

"I don't know, the note isn't signed, but based on what you've told me, I have reason to believe these photos were taken by him as well."

"Do you need us to leave so you can look at them, Hannah?" Isaac asked quietly.

Hannah wasn't sure what to say. She wasn't anxious to be alone with the sheriff and the pictures. But she didn't want to force Jenny to see something that might upset her . . . and she felt funny having Isaac see something that might be very private.

"Actually, I was thinking maybe you should wait to see them, Hannah," Sheriff Brewer said. "It might be best if we wait until your parents are free to join you."

Ben stared at her. "Is that what you want?"

She didn't want any of this. She didn't want to be nervous and frightened again. She didn't want to be standing in a sheriff's office. And she sure didn't want to be preparing herself to look at a bunch of pictures of herself that were certain to make her uncomfortable.

But even more than all of that, Hannah realized she didn't want to wait several more hours to return to this office to do this very same thing.

"I don't want to wait for my parents," she said. "I'm not a child and I don't need to be treated as such." Realizing that her imagination might be getting the best of her, she squeezed Isaac's arm. "Maybe you could look at them with me?"

"Of course I will."

"Do you think that's wise, Hannah?" Jenny asked. "If it is like the picture in Berlin, it's inappropriate."

"I know, but I survived many people seeing that photo before. If it's another like that, I'll survive it again. Also, Isaac is older. I won't worry about him being upset."

"I'm not that young. I want to see them, too."

"I've made up my mind, Jen."

Before her sister could argue again, Sheriff Brewer interrupted. "I think it might be best if Isaac stays. If only Isaac stays."

"We'll wait out here, then," Ben said. Though her sister looked disappointed, she followed him

166

and Sam out of the room. Hannah didn't like seeing Jenny upset, but resolutely pushed that worry away. This wasn't a time to worry about whether her siblings were sad that they were missing out on a special show-and-tell.

After the door closed, Hannah approached the desk. "I'm ready now."

New respect lit the sheriff's gaze. "Yes, I can see that you are." Since he still had on his gloves, he opened the envelope and without any fanfare, he placed all four items in front of her and Isaac, setting each out like playing cards.

The note was much like the others, except the size of each letter was bigger. Much bigger.

Together, the six letters sent a chilling message.

NO MORE

Hannah's mouth went dry as she forced herself to look at the three photos placed next to the note. They were in black-and-white, and five-by-seven in measurements.

But instead of photos of just herself, they were of her and Isaac. One was when they were walking; she was smiling up at him. Obviously amused by something he had said.

The next showed Isaac staring at her when they were outside Maggie's house. He looked serious and thoughtful. And she had her back to him, talking to Maggie.

When she finally allowed herself to gaze at the last photo, she understood why Sheriff Brewer hadn't wanted her to see the photos. It was taken when Isaac had hugged her. But instead of leaving the photo alone, Trent had drawn dark X's all over it, along with the words YOU WILL PAY at the bottom.

She gasped. The effect was dark and disturbing. In many ways, even more disturbing than the picture he'd taken of her in her bedroom.

She could also feel Isaac tense beside her.

Sheriff Brewer looked from one person to the other. "You didn't mention writing on the previous photos. Was there any?"

"*Nee.* They were only photos of me."

"I guess he's not pleased that I'm seeing Hannah," Isaac murmured.

"I'd call that an understatement," the sheriff said.

Hannah didn't speak. She couldn't seem to do anything but look at the photos. She was both creeped out by the photos . . . and caught up in the way she and Isaac looked. There was something soft, sincere, and intimate about the way they were gazing at each other.

They truly were a couple. It was like she'd been in a relationship but hadn't actually realized it. The photos showed the growth in their romance that she'd been ignoring.

While she continued to stare, Isaac spoke. "Is

this enough to get a restraining order issued for Hart County?"

"I'm not sure if it is. Since there's no name or address and none of you have seen him well enough to identify him without a doubt, it might be difficult to do."

"What can you do, then?"

"I'm going to call your sheriff in Berlin and get some more information," he said. After glancing at Isaac and Hannah again, he gathered up the photographs and slipped them back in the envelope. "After I talk to them and we see if we can find any fingerprints on any of this, I'll stop by and speak with you, Hannah. Okay?"

She nodded.

As he stood up, he said, "Is there any special reason you were so adamant about your parents not coming here today?"

"There are a lot of reasons," she said softly.

Holding out his hand for her to shake, Sheriff Brewer said, "I know this is difficult, but I want you to keep your faith. I'm not going to sit back and let you be terrorized anymore."

"Do you want Hannah to stay inside from now on?" Isaac asked.

"Hannah, that's up to you. However, I'm of the mind that you need to live your life. The worst thing that can happen to you is to be held captive by this creep and his camera."

That made her smile. "I suspect you are right."

"Don't give him any more encouragement, Hannah. Live your life. Walk with your boyfriend. Hang out with your friends. Smile. If you do all that, then all his pictures are going to be of you being happy."

Isaac wrapped his arm around her shoulders. "I'm going to be honest. A part of me likes that he took photos of the two of us. I like that he knows we are a couple, and I love that he knows you are no longer alone. It's not just you against him anymore, Hannah."

Both the sheriff's words and Isaac's comments made her feel a lot better. They were right. She needed to have faith . . . and she needed to revel in the fact that she wasn't alone.

She'd made a choice to stop hiding, and she felt stronger than ever before.

Chapter 17

Wednesday, August 3

"Do you two think Mamm and Daed will be home when we get there?" Ben asked after the three of them said goodbye to Isaac and Sam at the halfway point between their two houses.

While Jenny simply shrugged, Hannah said, "I hope so, but your guess is as good as mine." She hoped they were. She wanted to get this news—and their reaction to it—over with.

They walked further along. The sky was a pale blue and the last chill of the weather had finally passed. It was a perfect day to spend outside. Hannah noticed that more flowers had bloomed over the last week. She especially loved the daffodils and the tulips. Anything that was merry and bright. They lifted her spirits and reminded her that something beautiful could always be found around every corner, if one waited long enough.

She was just about to point out a particularly pretty grouping of pink daffodils when Jenny spoke up.

"Hey, Hannah?"

"Yeah?" she asked, thinking about her mother's garden, that maybe Mamm should plant some pansies or snapdragons, or something new and bright outside the kitchen windows. Something to bring a little beauty into our home.

"You really like Isaac, don't ya?"

"*Jah*. I like him a lot."

"What if things between you get even more serious?"

Hannah looked at Jenny curiously. "What if they do?"

"What happens then?" Her bottom lip trembled. "I mean, what do you think will happen to us?"

All thoughts of spring and rejuvenation faded away. "You mean if I marry him?" She pushed away the knee-jerk reaction of saying that she wasn't going to marry Isaac any time soon. Jenny's feelings were more important. "Why worry about what is going to happen to you?"

"Because you look after us," Jenny said, for once looking vulnerable instead of bulldoggish. "If you leave, then we'll be home alone."

Hannah paused, half waiting for Ben to say that Jenny was worrying about nothing. But instead, he appeared to be just as worried.

"Not really. Mamm and Daed will be there. They are occupied now, but they haven't given up being our parents."

"But if Daed dies, Mamm might not want to stay here," Ben said. "She probably won't."

"And I just got used to being here," Jenny blurted. "I don't want to go back to Ohio."

"You don't?" Hannah asked.

Jenny shook her head. "I'm different now. Aren't you?"

"I guess I am. I'm stronger."

"I think you are a lot stronger," Ben said. "And I've made friends here. But Mamm ain't all that happy."

Hannah felt as if this day's events were accompanied by a steamroller. Each topic was exhausting and felt like a minefield. "If Daed dies, then Mamm will stay here. Don't forget, that's why they bought this house in the first place. So Mamm would have a home where she didn't have to worry about the bills and the mortgage."

But instead of looking reassured, Ben exchanged glances with Jenny. Then he spoke. "We're pretty sure Mamm won't want to stay."

"Why would you say such a thing?"

"Mamm is lonely here."

"No, she isn't," she protested. "Mamm has that new job."

"Mamm has a new job that she doesn't like," Jenny corrected. "There's a difference."

"I know that." Stumbling around her words, she said, "Are you sure? I mean, she just got those flowers. And she mentions work a lot. She acts like she's happy about it."

"She's only acting happy because she knows Daed feels guilty, about being so sick."

It seemed like every conversation turn was a tangled maze of secrets and disclosures. "I didn't realize Daed felt that way." Feeling guiltier than ever, she said, "I'm sorry, you two. I didn't mean to make you feel so alone. I'll try harder."

After exchanging another look with his sister, Ben said, "If Mamm moves back and you marry Isaac, can I live with you instead of moving back to Ohio? I promise I won't be a lot of trouble."

"Don't talk like that. We shouldn't be talking about Daed dying or Mamm wanting to leave. It's not right."

"So is that a no?"

Growing more flustered by the second, she shook her head. "Of course it's not," she said quickly.

"Oh," he said. His voice was filled with dejection.

Realizing that Ben needed her to give him an answer, she gave him the only one she could. "Ben, if I do marry Isaac, and if our father does die, and if Mamm really doesn't want to live here and moves to Ohio, then yes, of course, you may move in with me and Isaac. Jenny, you too. Neither of you ever have to ask about something like that. I'll always want you near me."

"Okay, then," Ben said.

"*Danke*, Hannah," Jenny said.

They had been really worried. Goodness, but this conversation was awkward. She felt like she was already being their parent, and felt completely unprepared to be a *good* parent for them. "We should probably keep this conversation between the three of us," she said. "I don't want Mamm and Daed to know we talked about such things."

"Of course we're not going to mention it, Hannah," Ben said. "But things happen even when we don't want them to."

How did her siblings get so wise? She couldn't dispute anything they said. But even though they were growing up quickly, she knew they still needed reassurance and support.

"Ben, Jenny, please remember that it ain't a good idea to go around worrying about the future. One never knows what will happen. Ain't so?

Therefore, all that worrying simply becomes a waste of time."

"Don't you get it, Hannah?" Jenny asked as they approached their house and saw that the front door was open. "We have to worry about the future. Everything is going to happen sooner or later. A person can either be ready for it . . . or not."

Walking up the driveway, Hannah said, "If what you say is true, Jenny, let's hope that all this talking has prepared us for what is about to come."

Jenny heaved a sigh. "I don't think any of us is going to be ready for this."

An hour later, as the five of them sat around the kitchen table, Hannah reflected that Jenny had been exactly right. Her parents were not pleased.

Not about anything that had happened.

"You shouldn't have gone to the sheriff's office, Hannah," their father said. "You certainly had no right to drag your younger brother and sister along. That was irresponsible."

"First of all, there was no way I was going to wait to contact the authorities again. Secondly, I didn't drag them. They wanted to go."

"There was no way we were going to let her go alone, Daed," Ben said.

Her father glared at Hannah. "You are supposed to be shielding Ben and Jenny from activities like that."

"Going to the sheriff's office wasn't an activity. I went to report that Trent was sending me photographs again."

Her mother fussed with the silverware that was left on the table. "I don't think I can handle moving again."

"Sheriff Brewer is going to take care of things," Jenny said.

"He said he's going to stop Trent," Ben added. "He said Hannah shouldn't have to be so scared all the time."

Looking exhausted, their father nodded. "He is right. Hannah certainly does deserve to live a more peaceful life."

"Where were you today?" Jenny asked. "None of us knew."

After a slight pause, Mamm said, "We went to a new *doktah*."

"Are you going to get treatment now, Daed?" Hannah asked hopefully.

"*Nee*. But I did want to get some medicine and talk to them about what I might be facing in the next couple of months. And what your mother needs to expect."

"You're only worried about Mamm?" Jenny asked.

"Jenny, don't," Hannah said as she stood up. "We don't need to go there."

"I believe we have all said enough today," Daed said. "I need to rest."

Jenny stood up as well. "I'll help you with the dishes."

Hannah felt their parents' relief that the conversation was over. It was just as well. Nothing that could have been shared would have made any of them happier or more at ease with what was going to take place.

It seemed Jenny was right. The future came, whether one wished for it or not.

Chapter 18

Monday, August 8

For some reason, being back at the library studying didn't feel as hard as it had when Jenny had been so angry at her sister. She no longer resented studying geography and history. She no longer ignored Hannah's advice about learning to speak and write English properly.

Actually, now that several days had passed, Jenny was starting to think of the time she had to study as a gift.

Talking honestly with Hannah had helped Jenny become more settled. Because she and Ben had a better understanding of all that their older sister had endured, Jenny wasn't constantly fighting all the changes that had taken place. Coming clean about her communication with Trent had helped, too.

Even knowing that the sheriff, Sam, and Isaac were concerned helped Jenny's frame of mind. Her family wasn't trying to tackle every problem by themselves now. They were part of a larger group.

At last, she was starting to feel like herself again. It was nice to remember that the world around her wasn't as dark or as dreary as she'd been imagining it was.

Munfordville, Kentucky, wasn't Berlin, Ohio, but it was filled with good, caring people who were willing to accept her. They'd wanted her to join their community and be her friend, too. Even when their first impression of her had been that she'd had a giant chip on her shoulder.

In the two hours that she'd been at the library that evening, Jenny had smiled at several girls and even talked to a few of them. When others had noticed her smiling in a friendly way, they'd joined in conversation, too. It had been fun to feel so carefree.

Jenny could hardly remember the last time she'd felt so optimistic about the future. Months, most likely. Even back in Berlin, she'd had the feeling that something wasn't quite right in their lives.

It was ironic that now that so much was wrong with their lives, she felt happier than ever. She could only guess that it had to do with the fact that none of them were harboring a collection of dark secrets anymore.

She would have never guessed that knowing what was truly bad was actually a whole lot better than pretending that something was good.

After studying her geography terms for another ten minutes, she closed her notebook and smiled. And almost giggled.

Cole noticed. "What are you laughing about?" he asked as he took the seat next to her.

Today, Cole was wearing a short-sleeved light-green cotton shirt. She tried not to notice that it set off his eyes under his tortoiseshell frames. "Hello to you, too," she teased.

His eyebrows rose. "Hello."

Realizing he was still waiting for her to answer his question, she said, "I'm sorry, I forgot what you asked."

Cole was looking more puzzled by the second. "I asked what you were giggling about. I mean, if you want to share."

"It wasn't anything specific. I was just thinking that I was happy."

He smiled slightly as he squinted. And continued to give her a look like she was a confusing puzzle he was trying to piece together. "You seem different."

After making sure that they weren't being overheard, she nodded and smiled. "I guess I am." Straightening her shoulders a bit, she said, "Actually, I feel different. Almost like a new person."

"What happened?"

"I finally ironed some things out with my family."

He nodded in an understanding way. "You mean you talked with your sister?"

"*Jah*. Me and my sister finally talked about some things that had been bothering me," she said. "Hannah shared some other things, too. Now that I understand her better, I realize that I shouldn't have been so hard on her. It wasn't fair of me to fault her for acting the way she did."

"What happened to her?"

Though she ached to talk about everything that had been going on with someone, she hesitated. "I don't think I should share exactly what happened," she admitted slowly. "It's a pretty private thing. All I can say is that someone who used to be out of her life is back in. We're all going to rally around her and stop him from bothering her this time."

"Him?" He exhaled. "So, she's just having man troubles."

"It was way more than that." Deciding to share a little bit more because she couldn't bear the idea that Cole thought Hannah was overreacting because of a simple romantic squabble, Jenny said, "She'd made friends with a man who wouldn't leave her alone. He stalked her. It wasn't good."

"Wow."

Jenny stilled. "Why are you looking at me like that? Do you not believe that men can be stalkers or something?"

His eyes widened. "No, it's not that. I was just thinking that for a while there, I thought you were facing the same kind of situation."

His comment seemed like it came out of nowhere. "I've never even had a boyfriend. I don't know any boy well enough for him to want to start following me around or causing me trouble."

"Yeah. I guess not."

But there was something in his voice that made her think he was keeping a thought to himself. "You sure?"

"Yeah. It sounds so stupid now." Looking sheepish, he said, "See, for a while there, I thought Shane was your stalker."

A shudder went through her. "Shane? Why would you say that?"

"He was always looking for you. He wanted to know all about you, too. Especially things like how often you were coming in here, and where else you went."

"He . . . he did all that?"

Cole shrugged. "Listen, I'm probably making too much of everything. You should just ignore me."

"*Nee*, I'm glad you are sharing, Cole." As a stronger feeling of foreboding coursed through her, she asked hesitantly, "Um, when Shane asked you those things, what would you tell him?"

"Nothing much. I mean, it's not like I knew your schedule or knew where you were all the time. But it was odd, you know? Sometimes he'd say a certain word or look a little panicked or on edge. It was like he was really missing you. And your sister, too, of course."

"My sister?" It was a struggle to keep her voice steady. "He asked about Hannah?"

"Well, yeah." He shrugged. "But I guess that's normal, on account of him and her being such good friends and all."

She felt a wave of uneasiness but pushed it away. Surely, the things she was thinking couldn't be true. "He must have been really confused. My sister has never met Shane."

Cole pushed his glasses back up the bridge of his nose. "Sure she did. I might not have known where you were, but I remember my conversations with him. Why, Shane talked about Hannah all the time."

"What did he say?"

"He said they used to be real close in Berlin. That she hung out in the library there, too. Just like you are, here. It must be a pattern with you Hilty girls," he teased.

Warning bells went off inside her. "He knew that Hannah liked the library?"

"Oh, for sure." He paused, drummed his hands on his knee. "Shane said he used to go to the restaurant where she worked. He missed her." He smiled, looking a little embarrassed. "I don't know why I'm telling you all of this now."

"I wish you would have told me he said all that earlier."

"I don't know why I didn't." Cole flushed. "I guess I was a little jealous, if you want to know the truth. He knew you so well, it made me think I would never have a chance with you."

"That's sweet of you to say, but I didn't know him well."

A line formed between his brows. "Sure you did. He knew everything about Hannah, and he told me that he intended to know you real well, too."

"He never talked to me about Hannah," she said slowly. "When did you see him last?"

"Yesterday. He said he had a delivery to make, then he was going to get out of here for a couple of days."

Jenny felt like her heart was about to stop. "He had a delivery?"

"*Jah*. Then, he asked me to tell ya that he hadn't forgotten about you. Just in case you were worried that he had, or something."

She pressed a hand to her chest. "Just in case," she whispered.

Cole stepped closer. "Were you worried about that, Jenny?" he asked. "Have you gotten really close?"

"*Nee*! I—I mean, I already decided I didn't like

hanging out with him," she said in a choked voice. "He was kinda old."

"Does this mean that the two of us can now hang out together? Because I would like that."

"Sure. Of course we can. I'd like that, too. You are a really nice person, Cole. I'm sorry I didn't act friendly from the start."

Just as Cole was about to tell her something else, his focus shifted to something behind her. "Sorry, but I gotta go. Those are some buddies of mine. They've been waiting for me outside. I guess they got tired of waiting."

Jenny turned to see a group of four Amish boys all standing next to the open door and grinning at Cole like they were very amused by something he was doing. When they noticed her looking at them, the tallest one waved. She smiled at him and waved back, just as the librarian folded her arms over her chest and glared at the teenaged interlopers.

Cole jumped to his feet. "Uh-oh. Miss Landry's gonna get mad. I better get them out of here. See you later."

"Okay."

After he took about four or five steps, he turned back to her. "Hey, will I see you at the sandwich sale?"

"I guess so. Are you going to go?"

He smiled. "Of course. It's a lot of fun. It's not just sandwiches, you know. They usually offer quilts and other items to auction off. One time, it was two tickets on a Pioneer Trails bus to Pinecraft."

"Wow. It sounds like a lot of fun."

"*Jah*. Everyone goes. It's a good way to see everyone, too. And it would be a real good opportunity for you to meet some more people. Wouldn't it?" He edged away a little further, then blurted, "Jenny, would you like to go with me and my friends?"

Nodding, she smiled. "*Danke.*"

"Want to meet here?"

"Can I just meet you there? I'll probably be with Ben."

"Sure. I'll look for you on Saturday."

"Cole Woods, stop talking," Miss Landry called out.

He blushed. "Sorry, Miss Landry," he said as he put on his hat. "Bye, Jenny. See you then."

She raised her hand. "*Jah*. See you then. And *danke*. Now you had better go before Miss Landry gets really mad."

"Yeah, you're right." He smiled again, this time even sweeter.

She smiled back, though she didn't know if she'd ever felt so sick to her stomach without having the flu.

After he walked out the door, Jenny groaned.

Miss Landry glared at her.

"Sorry," Jenny said and wandered to the book stacks, then headed toward a back corner where the librarian always stored a stepping stool. When she got to it, she sat down and reveled in the small sense of privacy she found there. Of the many times she'd come here and sought refuge in the stacks, no one had ever come around and bothered her. It was her own secret hiding place.

Now that she was certain that she wasn't being watched, Jenny rested her head in her hands and her elbows on her knees. She was essentially in a small ball. And she was glad of it. She would've hugged herself if she could.

Because everything that she was thinking wasn't good. Shane had seemed happy to get to know her. She'd been grateful for his attentions and sometimes had talked too much.

Now she realized that he'd encouraged her to talk about herself. He'd asked her questions about her family and about their old life in Berlin. He'd been so interested, and she'd been flattered.

But now she realized that he might have simply been using her to get even more information about Hannah.

She'd always assumed that she'd known who Trent was. But maybe she hadn't known him at all. After all, her parents had kept him a secret as much as they could.

And Hannah had acted like she never wanted to talk about Trent ever again.

Because of that, Jenny had imagined him to be a scary-looking sort of man. Difficult. Violent. But today, when Hannah had talked in the police station, Jenny had realized that Trent hadn't been like that at all. At first, he'd been nice and eager to please. Friendly and a good listener.

A lot like Shane.

No, *exactly* like Shane.

She might have been jumping to conclusions. Maybe she really was. Maybe Shane and Trent were two different people.

Maybe.

But if they weren't, then Jenny had done something completely unforgivable.

She'd allowed her sister's stalker into their lives again. Why, she'd practically gripped his hand and pulled him in. And now they were all paying the price.

Chapter 19

Tuesday afternoon, August 9

The fish weren't biting. Isaac figured that was just as well. He had a lot on his mind, and he would much rather attend to his worries than reel in some unlucky fish.

But as one hour passed into two, Isaac still wasn't sure what to do about Hannah. He wanted to protect her and solve all her problems at the same time.

He also felt the need to analyze his feelings for her. He wasn't exactly proud of this, but everything about Hannah caught him off guard. He'd never met a woman who was so complicated. Learning about her past and the things that she'd had to deal with was eye opening. He felt naïve next to her.

Part of him also wondered if he was a good match for her. After all, he was basically a simple man. He had lived in one town all of his life and had a job that he'd learned from a trusted uncle. Until he'd met Hannah, most of his worries had revolved around his family or a small, select group of people he knew well.

Now he was going to sheriff's office and conversing about stalkers and photographs and laws and restraining orders. It wasn't that he blamed Hannah for any of it. He didn't.

But he also wasn't sure if he wanted to tackle such worldly problems. Even thinking of such things made him feel guilty.

"I canna decide if you are getting the best of the fish or those fish are getting the best of you," his father called out.

Turning to watch his father approach through the weeds and grass in his thick-soled leather boots, Isaac said, "I'd say it was the fish, though I'm not real anxious to clean any."

His father chuckled. "You never have been, boy." Walking to his side, he held out a hand.

"Give me that rod and reel. I might as well catch us some supper while we talk."

Though Isaac wasn't all that sure he wanted to sit on the creek bed and chat with his father, he handed off the pole without argument. Once his father claimed the fishing pole, he reeled it in, checked the hook, then at last released the line with a smooth flick of his wrist. Mamm always said that Daed could make a good amount of money teaching others to fly-fish, but Daed had always said it wasn't the job for him.

Isaac had wondered if he was more worried about the teaching or the fact that he would turn his favorite hobby into a job.

After a few minutes, his father pulled out a familiar blue-and-red wrapper, opened it up, and popped a piece of gum in his mouth. "Don't tell Mamm," he said before chomping down with a look of pure bliss.

Isaac shifted but said nothing. The fact was that their mother knew Daed liked his Bazooka bubble gum. She'd always known it for as long as Isaac could remember.

Years ago, she'd confided to Isaac and Maggie that their father had once had a powerful addiction to chewing tobacco. He'd started chewing gum as a way of ending that addiction. However, now he was as addicted to that as he'd been to the tobacco.

It remained his father's secret, hidden vice. No one in the family had ever had the desire to ruin his secret, so they'd all pretended that it wasn't happening.

After another five minutes passed in silence, Daed reeled in the line, then swung it out again.

The hook and line flew out over the creek like a fragile bird in flight, plunging into the rolling creek with a small splash.

"You know, it always surprises me when I find you here, Isaac. I would have thought you would have found an activity that you liked better, to help you clear your mind."

"I don't dislike fishing, Daed."

"It's just that you don't like it much. Come now. We know it's more than just an aversion to cleaning scales."

Isaac laughed. "You're right. But it does relax me. I like the quiet."

"Me, too," Daed said as he swung out his arm again, smiling as the line made a perfect arc. After blowing a bubble, he cracked his gum and settled back in. "This is why I never wanted to give fishing lessons. Here, on the creek bed, I can do what I want. I can blow bubbles, watch the water, and listen and watch all the beauty that the Lord has given me."

His father's comment had a lot of truth to it. With a start, Isaac realized that it had a lot to do with what he'd been thinking about when his father had walked up. "We are blessed. Sometimes I fear that I take it all for granted."

"You sound bothered by that."

"I'm not. But I don't want to forget to count my blessings."

"We'd all be walking around with silly smiles on our faces if we only thought about how good things were all the time," his father said with a grimace. "And that would make us all look ridiculous. Ain't so?"

Isaac bit back a smile of his own. "Indeed, Father."

"It's not taking something for granted if you are feeling happy with your life."

"I guess you heard about what I did today. What Sam and I did."

His father's gum cracked. "You heading up to the sheriff's office? *Jah*, I might have heard something about that."

"Are you upset that I took Samuel there? I suppose I should have asked you or Mamm for permission."

"Have you met your brother? I don't believe he would have stayed behind unless we locked him in his room. Besides, he was old enough."

"I've been sitting here thinking about Hannah and her siblings."

"And about her note?"

"Yes. And the pictures she received."

"Some had you in them, I hear," he said lightly. "*Jah*."

Daed reeled in the line, then with a flick of his

wrist, cast off again. "I don't know if I've ever had my picture taken."

"I'd be lying if I didn't take a good look at myself."

His father grinned. "What did you see?"

Isaac thought about that. "A man. A man who's bigger than I thought I was."

"That is who I see, too. I see you as strong and able, son. Maybe even a good protector. Maybe even a man who is better than he thinks he is."

Isaac liked that description, though he wasn't sure it fit him all that well. "Daed, I don't know if I'm the right man for Hannah Hilty."

"You ain't supposed to. That's what courting is for, son."

"She is nice. And sweet. And pretty."

"She is mighty pretty. Dark hair and hazel eyes are a striking combination. She's probably caused more than one man to take a look at her twice."

Isaac wasn't too thrilled about that. "I think I might really like her. *Nee*, no, what I'm trying to say is that I do like her a lot."

"That's *gut*. She is a nice Amish girl who lives close."

It would be so easy to act as if that was all that mattered to him. "I'm kind of worried that she has such a checkered past."

"Are you worried that she did something to deserve it?"

"Not at all." Thinking of that note, he shook his

head for emphasis. "She didn't deserve it at all, but . . ."

"But you are wondering if you want to take on all of her problems."

Isaac exhaled. "Yes. That is exactly what I'm thinking. She's also got a sick father. He has cancer."

"A lot for one girl to handle."

"Yes." Isaac shifted, hating how he sounded but feeling like he needed to be completely honest. "I like her and I am sure that she likes me, too. But I don't know if I am the man she needs. Maybe she needs someone more worldly."

"Yes, I can see how a man who has more experience with stalkers would be a better fit for Hannah."

Isaac gaped at his father. "Sometimes you say the craziest things."

There went the fishing line again. "Do I? Huh."

"All right. I get it. I guess that was a stupid thing to say. How about this? I don't know if I'm strong enough to take on all of her problems. I don't know if I want to."

The line twitched. Looking pleased, his father stood up and reeled it in slowly, gently guiding it toward him with the patience that only an experienced fisherman could have.

Isaac got to his feet as well. Watched the interplay between his father and that fish. Suddenly, the line jumped and the shadow of a bass slid away.

His father spun the reel. The hook was there, but the bait was gone. "Wily fish," his *daed* griped under his breath.

His eyes were twinkling, though.

"You don't look too disappointed, Daed."

"*Nee?*" He rubbed his beard. "Well, I guess I'm not. That fish was a fighter. Maybe even a bit smarter than the average bass."

Isaac grinned. "That was surely the reason he was able to beat you at your own game."

"Exactly." Daed methodically reeled in the rest of the line, straightening the thin fishing wire as he did so, inspecting it for snags.

"Are you done?"

"*Jah.* I think so. You've been out here a while. Your mother would probably like me to bring you home. Let's gather our things together and do chores." He paused. "And get Freeman out of her hair."

Isaac gathered up his cooler and net before taking the rod and reel from his father, disassembling it, then putting it back in its case. With a look of regret, his *daed* pulled out the gum wrapper, spit out his gum, then neatly folded it into a paper towel that he'd pulled out of a hidden pocket.

When they started walking, Isaac noticed that his father looked just as relaxed and at peace as he had when he'd first joined him. Though that made him happy, Isaac knew his father well enough to know that he'd come to the creek to do more than almost catch a fish.

"Hey, Daed?"

"Hmm?"

"Did you want to talk to me about something?"

His father adjusted his straw hat so it shielded his eyes a little better. "I thought we already did talk, son."

"I know we talked about Hannah and my feelings, but you didn't say much. Were you hoping to tell me what you thought?"

"I didn't do that?" His voice was thick with surprise. "Huh. I was fairly sure I did."

Isaac reviewed their conversation. Try as he might, he couldn't recall any useful words of wisdom. "Nope. You didn't."

As they turned toward the house and saw Sam glaring at Freeman, who was holding a kitten instead of a broom, his father grinned. "Looks like we're going to be helping out Samuel today instead of your mother. Freeman certainly does like to play, don't he?"

"Daed, what do you think I should do about Hannah?"

"Whatever you think is right, son. That is what I think you should do." Just as Isaac was about to ask him to be a bit more specific—okay, a whole lot more specific—his father raised a hand.

"Freeman?" When his little brother's head shot up, *Daed* called out, "Boy, are you making your *bruder* do all the work while you play with cats?"

"He is!" Sam shouted.

Freeman bit his bottom lip, but didn't let go of his kitten. "I was gonna help him, Daed. I truly was. In a minute."

Isaac stopped as he watched his father gently pull the kitten out of Freeman's arms and cradle it like a football. Then he pointed to the broom. "It's time, son. Don't like to see you watch others work. Understand?"

For a full two seconds, Freeman gazed at the kitten with longing before grabbing the broom. "*Jah*, Father. I understand."

Finally, it all became clear to Isaac. Life was full of ups and downs. Kittens and chores and friendships and family. It was uneven and unexpected. It was full of quiet moments and chewing gum and fish that got away.

Each was important in its own way. If he allowed Hannah's troubles to overshadow everything he admired about her, then he was doing both of them a disservice. Real, meaningful relationships were about so much more than smooth sailing.

Hannah was more than just a stalker's victim.

She was far more important to him than that.

Chapter 20

Saturday, August 20

"I don't know about you, but I need a break," Maggie said, taking off one of her plastic gloves in order to rub the middle of her back. "Hannah, how many sandwiches do you think we've made so far this morning?"

Looking down at the long metal table that they'd set up in the high school gym, Hannah whistled low. The table was almost covered with neatly wrapped sandwiches, or ones that were somewhere in the process of being put together and wrapped. "I couldn't begin to count them. Maybe a hundred?"

"It's got to be over that," Christina, Maggie's cousin, called out from her station by the plastic wrap. "I reckon it's closer to three hundred." Giggling softly, she continued. "At least, it feels that way."

They'd started making sandwiches around six that morning and had hardly stopped for breaks.

"I bet it's more than a mere three hundred. Maybe we made a thousand. Maybe ten thousand!" Maggie exclaimed with a big smile.

"I see your penchant for exaggeration is alive and well," Christina said sarcastically.

Maggie didn't look offended in the slightest. "I canna help but joke. It's either that or cry, since my back and shoulders feel like I've never done another thing in my life besides make ham-and-cheese sandwiches."

Maggie's comments were so outlandish, Hannah burst out laughing. "I've never heard such complaining!"

"I'm only stating how I feel," she said with a wink. "I didn't say it was the honest truth."

After taking a sip of her bottled water, Hannah picked up her knife and got busy slathering mustard on each piece of homemade bread again. She had a good system down now. She would spread brown mustard on five pieces of bread, then carefully place generous slices of ham on each.

Maggie would take over the next step. She would put cheese, lettuce, slices of tomato, and homemade sliced pickles on top of the ham. Finally, Christina and a lady named Violet wrapped the sandwiches in plastic wrap before finally placing them in the cooler.

Other people were putting together sacks with chips and homemade cookies in them. Still others were either preparing their booth or organizing volunteers to deliver sandwiches to people who had already placed orders. It was a huge undertaking.

There was a festive atmosphere all around them.

The gym was buzzing with activity as well as a strong feeling of anticipation among everyone involved. Hannah had never been a part of anything like this before, but she was so thankful for the experience. Not only were they going to help Darryl and Mercy, she'd gained some new friends. Maggie and Christina had already started talking about getting together in the future, but the next time, just for fun.

After stretching her arms above her head and draining the glass of lemonade she'd just poured from the iced pitcher near the gymnasium's door, Maggie said, "I guess I can't procrastinate any longer. We're going to need to finish up as quick as we can. Why, the benefit will begin in just two hours."

That announcement spurred everyone on. With a burst of energy, the other women went back to their posts, slipped on gloves, and got back to work.

After they'd put together another five or six sandwiches, Maggie smiled at her. "I have to tell ya that all of us are mighty impressed with you, Hannah Hilty."

"I don't know why." Actually, she would have thought everyone would be feeling everything but impressed with her. She'd been pretty shy the first couple of hours. She'd also started off making sandwiches a whole lot slower than the other girls, not wanting to mess anything up. "I haven't worked nearly as quickly as the rest of you have."

"Oh, we could care less about your sandwich-making abilities," Christina said.

"Oh?"

"Oh, for sure. No, we like how friendly you've been. And then, too, there's our fascination about your personal life."

"What about it?" A bolt of panic seared through her as she imagined the worst. Maybe they'd heard about Trent, too. Maybe Isaac had told everyone.

"Only that you've managed to snag the interest of one Isaac Troyer. He's been playing it cool and aloof for years now."

"Until you!" Violet quipped.

"We should also tell ya that a whole lot of us have tried to get his attention at one time or another," Christina said as she winked. "But no matter what we did or said, he was never anything but polite."

Looking over at Christina, Maggie winked. "Actually, we were starting to believe that his heart was never going to be spoken for. Until you came along."

Hannah wasn't sure if they were making it up, teasing her, or being serious. "I don't know that I have snagged his heart."

"I think you have," Christina said in her tinkling, high-pitched voice. "Whenever you are near, his gaze remains settled on ya. We've all noticed."

"Isaac is kind. He seems to be a good friend, too. He, um, has wanted me to get to know more people here and has helped me a lot." That was the heart of it, too, she thought. She feared that he felt guilty about the way they'd gotten to know each other and he was trying to make up for that.

"Our Isaac is definitely kind," Maggie agreed. "But that ain't how he's acting whenever he's around you. Now what I want to know is what you did to spark his interest." After grinning at the other girls, she said, "What's your secret, Hannah?"

"I have no idea." Honestly, what could she say to a comment like that?

"Maggie, stop," Christina chided. "You're embarrassing the poor girl. Besides, we know she is far more than just a pretty face. No doubt Isaac has noticed as many good things about her as we have."

While she and Isaac were now more than mere friends, Hannah wanted to hold their new relationship close to her heart. She liked the idea of there being something promising between just the two of them. "Isaac has been a good friend to me. He's gone out of his way to help his new neighbor. I'm grateful for his help."

Maggie sighed. "It's a shame you don't want to play along, but I'll leave you alone about it. For the record, I just wanted to let you know that we're real happy for you both. You are sweet and a *gut* addition to our community. You couldn't find a better man than Isaac Troyer, either. He's got a warm heart and he's fun, too." As she handed another sandwich down the row, she added, "It's obvious that Isaac couldn't be happier these days. Since he's often been alone and seemed a little distant, we know his new attitude is because of you."

Those heartfelt words meant the world to her. A part of her ached to share her past and to tell Maggie just what her kind comments meant to her and for what reason.

Instead, she said simply, "*Danke.* Isaac makes me happy, too. I feel blessed that the Lord rought us together."

"It is a blessing," Maggie said. "Sometimes I think it's easy to forget that the Lord wants us all to be happy and to follow His will." Glaring at the sandwiches, she said, "I need to take care to remember that more often. In between all of our business and plans, life happens."

Hannah thought she couldn't have said that better herself.

In one hour, all the sandwiches were done and they were cleaning up when Isaac joined them.

"Hannah, look who's here," Maggie said brightly. "Isaac!"

Hannah tucked her head to try to hide her smile.

Still grinning at him brazenly, Maggie said, "Did you come in here for a particular reason, Isaac? Do you need me to help ya with anything?"

Isaac paused, looked in confusion at Maggie and two other girls who were giggling, and then seemed to collect himself. "*Danke*, Maggie, but I came in here to check on Hannah."

"That's mighty nice of you. Ain't so, Hannah?"

Feeling sorry for Isaac, Hannah rushed around the table she was wiping down. "Don't mind them," she said as she got to his side. "They are teasing me."

He frowned. "Why would they be doing that?"

That question, of course, made her cheeks turn bright pink. "Never you mind. How are you?"

"Tired. And wet," he said, gesturing toward his shirt that she'd just noticed was very damp. "Paul and I have been setting up stations for ice. I'm afraid it ain't possible for me to carry buckets of ice and water without getting a good bit of it on myself."

"At least it's a cool job."

He grinned. "It is at that." Looking as aware as she that they were being watched, he leaned a little closer. "When the sale begins, do you have any plans?"

"Not really. I was just going to ask Maggie where she wanted me to help out next."

"I was hoping you'd say that. Want to stand with me at the drink table? Some other people are already going to be taking care of the money, but they need people to pull drinks out of the coolers, wipe them off, and hand them out. Want to do that with me?"

"I'd be happy to."

Looking pleased, he nodded. "Great. Come find me when you are ready. I'll be outside looking for you."

"Okay."

Smiling softly, he leaned a little closer. He looked like he was tempted to say something else when he glanced just beyond her. Then, with a wry shake of his head, he abruptly turned around and strode out.

Confused, Hannah frowned at his retreating form, then realized what had set him off when all of the girls around her burst into laughter.

"It's so *gut* to see how kind Isaac treats the new members of our community, Hannah," Maggie said.

"Wonderful-*gut*," Violet said. "Heartwarming, even."

"Now we know who my mother should ask to be in charge of next year's welcome-wagon committee," Christina chirped. "I've yet to see a member be so attentive."

Hannah pressed her hands to her cheeks in a poor attempt to hold off another blush. "You girls are terrible! I know he didn't know how to handle your teasing. I think you embarrassed him." She knew they certainly had embarrassed her!

"Oh, don't worry about our Isaac," Christina said. "He might seem flustered around you, but that's not his usual way. He takes everything in stride on account of him almost dying and all. A little bit of ribbing ain't going to bother him in the slightest."

Almost dying? "What did you say?"

Christina turned serious. "Has Isaac not told you about what happened to him when he was thirteen?"

"*Nee.*" She was tempted to ask for the whole story but decided that that was definitely a story for Isaac himself to share.

As if she was reading Hannah's mind, Christina said, "I'm sure he'll talk to you about that when the time is right. And then, well, you'll understand why we're all so happy for him now. And for you, too, of course," she said before she went back to help Maggie load up sandwiches into a cooler.

Picking up the cloth, Hannah ran it along the table again. But her mind certainly wasn't on that task. Instead, she was thinking about Isaac's easy smiles. His patience. The way he was so amiable and generally happy.

Had she just learned the reason for his positive attitude?

If so, she realized that they had something in common. They'd both fought something that had threatened to harm them, that had been unexpected and unwarranted. But while she'd reacted by withdrawing from the world, Isaac had seemed to embrace everything like it was a gift.

There was something to be said for that. Something that she needed to learn how to do, even if it took weeks and months.

Chapter 21

Saturday, August 20

Looking at Hannah as she walked out to join him, Isaac decided that it was official: women really were a mystery to him. Hannah had been working in a hot un-air-conditioned gymnasium for at least five hours. During that time, she'd set up the assembly line, made hundreds of sandwiches, and then cleaned it all up, too. She should look tired and rumpled.

Yet, here she was, walking to his side, with hardly a hair out of place.

He, on the other hand, felt as sweaty as he no doubt looked. He was beginning to be real thankful that he'd gotten so soaked with his ice duty. Maybe it helped him not be too smelly.

Yeah, right. That was surely wishful thinking.

"Isaac, you look like you are concentrating on something mighty important," Hannah said.

"Are you having some trouble with the drinks?"

"Not at all. I was just standing here thinking about the differences between men and women."

Her eyes widened. "I see."

Suddenly realizing that she could be imagining all sorts of things, he blurted, "I was thinking about how fresh you appear. As opposed to me."

To his relief, she grinned. "You do look like you have been a hard-working man."

"I'm hoping I don't smell too badly."

"If you do smell, I'll, um, try to deal with it as best I can. I wouldn't worry about it, anyway. I'm fairly sure I smell like lunch meat." Wrinkling her nose, she added, "I don't think I want to have a ham sandwich for a couple of weeks."

"We've got a few minutes. Do you want to walk around a bit?"

"Of course," she said with a smile.

He smiled back, liking her carefree answer. Hannah was really coming out of her shell around him, and he was so glad of that. He wanted to get to know the real her, not just the guarded person she'd been that first day by the creek. Of course, he also wanted to be able to share more of himself without feeling like he was walking on eggshells.

Around them, the crowd grew.

The high school soccer field and parking lot were packed with people and cars, and even more buggies. People of all ages were milling around, too. Some were simply doing what he and Hannah were doing, talking and looking. Others were taking care of last-minute setup.

As was their way, teenagers and grade-school children were racing or weaving through all the crowds. It made it a bit of a challenge to walk anywhere. One needed to constantly be looking right and left before stepping forward.

Isaac didn't want Hannah to get nervous, so he made sure to stay close to her. Realizing that she might be uncomfortable with the large crowd, since she'd been so skittish just a few weeks previously, he did his best to check on her continually.

"Let me know if this is all too much for you," he said. "I don't want you to feel overwhelmed."

"I would have thought this would have scared me an awful lot, but I seem to be doing okay." Smiling at him, she said, "It must be the company."

He liked that. He liked that she felt safe and secure by his side. He liked that he was able to be someone that she felt she could depend on. "Thank you for that," he said.

As they walked on, she said, "Isaac, Christina mentioned something about you that I didn't know."

"Oh? What was that?"

"You don't have to talk about it, if you don't want to," she said in a rush. "But, well, she said that you almost died once."

He turned to examine her face. "That is true."

"Is it a secret?"

"It ain't a secret. Sorry if I seem to be taken aback. It's because I am surprised you hadn't already heard." After taking a moment to figure out how to tell her what happened, he shrugged his shoulders, thinking that the storytelling didn't really matter all that much. "You see, when I was thirteen, I got real sick. I had spinal meningitis. I was in the hospital for quite some time."

"I've never heard of that."

"Most people haven't, I don't think. My parents sure didn't. Doctors, of course, know the symptoms, but since it starts out with an assortment of aches and pains and a fever, my parents didn't take me in right away. By the time they did, it was almost too late."

Her eyes widened. "That had to have been mighty frightening."

"It was." It didn't take much for him to remember the pain and the panic that had accompanied the realization that nothing his mother was doing for him made a lick of difference. "I remember being so sick and weak and hurting so bad that I thought dying was going to be a blessing."

"But after they got you to the hospital, you got better. Right?"

"I did, after about a scary twenty-four hours." Seeing that she looked so worried, practically like she might pass out, he patted her shoulder. "Don't look so upset. I'm fine now."

"I know. I was just thinking about your parents and your siblings. I bet they were afraid that they'd lose you."

"They were. But you know how things are, right? After the fact, it's so easy to think about reactions and put everything into perspective. When it happens, though . . ." His voice drifted off as he shuddered.

"When it happens, all you think about is getting through the moment."

He nodded. "That's right." Since it was almost time for them to get to their assigned station, he attempted to finish up his story on a good note. "Now, looking back, well, I wouldn't give up that experience for the world."

"I find that hard to believe."

"It's true." As when remembering that journey in the hospital often did, Isaac felt his voice warm and become more expansive. He doubted he'd ever be able to convey just how much his brush with death had changed him, but he kept attempting to put it into clumsy words.

"It made me appreciate everything a little bit more," he said. "It made me not worry about things that don't matter."

"Yes, I can see how stewing on small things might seem silly after everything you went through."

"It wasn't that as much as the realization that I was changed. Facing the fear that I might not live to see another week made me look at every day afterward a little differently, too." Staring out across the crowded parking lot, he said, "It gave me hope, too. Because if I can come through that with a stronger faith and believe in the love of my family and friends, I can get through anything."

"I'm so glad I asked about that. Isaac, you are such an inspiration."

"Not so much. I mean, look what you've been going through."

When she didn't reply, he turned to her. "Hannah?"

But instead of answering, she was standing still, frozen. She looked scared, too. As scared as he'd been when he'd thought he was going to die.

"Hey, are you all right? Did my story upset you?"

When she didn't respond, he moved closer. Stepped to his right so that he was facing her all while he was trying to recall what he'd exactly said. "Hannah? Hannah, what is it?"

Still no answer.

Now he was growing concerned. What was wrong with her? What had he said that would trigger such a response?

It took another few seconds, but finally she came back to herself. She licked her bottom lip. Tried to get her bearings, then blurted, "He's here. Trent is here. I just saw him."

As a chill went through him, Isaac suddenly realized he'd just spouted a mouthful of lies.

Until this very moment, he hadn't known what real terror actually was.

Chapter 22

Saturday, August 20

Isaac grabbed her arm. "Hannah, are you sure?" he asked, his voice as intense as his grip.

She was sure. And was finding her ability to speak far more difficult an undertaking. Actually, even breathing seemed to be an effort. From the moment she'd seen Trent's familiar form, walking through the crowd like he belonged there, she'd felt as if the wind had been knocked out of her.

And with that blow, the memories returned. Next thing she knew, she was back in Ohio, back in Berlin, being frightened to death. Every scattered emotion she'd experienced returned to her—from the way she'd become afraid of windows, to the embarrassment that she'd been targeted, to the trepidation she'd felt that the stalking would never be over.

All of those thoughts had become her constant companions.

Still clutching her arm, Isaac was scanning

the area. "Where was he? Do you see him still?"

Isaac's intense tone brought her back to the present. Instead of pointing, she tried to gather her thoughts. "I don't see him anymore. But just a few minutes ago, I know I saw him in the crowd. He wasn't walking. He was staring at us."

"What is he wearing?"

She was still so shaken up, Hannah closed her eyes and tried to focus on the Trent she'd just seen, not the one who haunted her dreams.

"He has on a yellow shirt," she said at last. "And jeans." As she swallowed, she remembered one more thing. "And a black ball cap."

Isaac nodded. "That's *gut*, Hannah. You remembered a lot." His voice was reassuring and even. "Now, are you sure he saw you? There are a lot of Amish girls here in blue dresses. I have a feeling you wouldn't stick out like he does. After all, he's an Englisher in a bright-yellow shirt and black baseball cap."

"I have no doubt that he saw me. He was looking directly at me, Isaac. At you, too." A shiver ran through her. "I am certain that is why he came to this sale, Isaac."

"I wonder why he didn't come over here and talk to you."

"That isn't what he's about." Though it was a struggle, Hannah attempted to describe Trent's nature. "He likes playing a game with me, Isaac. He likes knowing that I am nervous and on edge.

Afraid. It's what he does. He follows me, then darts away."

"He sounds like the worst sort of man." He let go of her arm and ran his hand down his face. Grimacing, he continued. "Actually, this Trent sounds even worse than that, but I don't want to offend your ears."

He sounded so disgruntled, Hannah felt like smiling. "I doubt you could think anything about him that I haven't thought before."

His gaze warmed before he looked out into the crowd again. "Did you see him do anything else?"

"*Nee*. I looked into the crowd and saw him stare right back at me. After a second or so, he glanced your way, and he didn't look happy."

"*Gut*. I'm not too happy with him, either."

Isaac's concern for her was sweet, but she knew he would be no match for Trent. Trent was taller and weighed at least thirty more pounds than he did. But more than that, there was a dangerous edge to him. How could anyone as good as Isaac fight that?

Realizing that Trent might very well go after Isaac next, viewing him as a rival, Hannah reached out and gripped his arm. "I'm so sorry. This is terrible. I'm putting you in danger, too. Maybe we should separate."

"Absolutely not."

"But you could get hurt."

"I can handle myself *and* look after you,

Hannah," he said quietly as he moved his hand to the small of her back. "Here is what we are going to do. We are going to get out of here right away. I'm going to take you to Sheriff Brewer's office and you are going to tell him what you saw."

"I don't think my restraining order stands here. Maybe he'll get mad that I'm bothering him again."

"Don't you remember how Sheriff Brewer reacted? He doesn't want you hurt. He took you seriously. You don't have to prove anything to him. He's going to be glad you talked to him."

"What if Trent comes to my house?" she asked quickly, her voice sounding sharp even to her ears. "What if my parents or Jenny and Ben are in danger?"

He hated that she was so upset. If they lived in a different world, or if they knew each other better, he would have taken her in his arms and held her close. He might have even kissed her until she stopped talking and finally relaxed.

But of course that wasn't who they were, or that type of couple. Therefore, he attempted to ease her mind the best he could as he kept weaving her through the crowd. "Hannah, if he is leaving things at your doorstep, he already knows where you live."

"You are right." Giving herself a little shake, she said, "Honestly, what am I doing? When am I going to be able to get myself under control?"

"You are doing fine," he murmured as he guided

her past the edge of the parking lot, never letting go of her arm. There were far less people around, which eased him, yet also made him a little wary, too.

If they weren't nestled in the safety of numbers, she was going to be more at risk. He hated that.

"Don't be so hard on yourself," he said when they reached a quiet street that was only two blocks away from the sheriff's office. "Remember, Trent is the one who is at fault. Not you. Never you."

She nodded as she drew in a ragged breath. "Yes. You are right. I am sorry."

"Oh, Hannah. You must stop apologizing," he whispered. Then, because he was ordering her around again, and because he knew she was on the verge of tears, he let himself do what he'd wanted to do for days. He pulled her into his arms.

Placing her hands on his biceps, her lips parted. "Isaac?"

"Just relax. Let me help you. Let me hold you. None of this is your fault. You didn't do anything to deserve this man's games. Okay?"

"Okay," she repeated, but it didn't look like she believed him.

He tried again. Softening his tone, he added, "I am not leaving you, Hannah. You are no longer alone. I've got you."

After another second passed, she leaned into his embrace.

When he felt her relax, Isaac felt as if he'd just won a fierce battle. He had no idea what was going to happen next, but at last she was allowing him to help her.

As Hannah pressed her cheek against Isaac's chest, she tried to get her bearings again. Closing her eyes, she prayed for guidance and prayed for strength. She wanted to fight. She wanted to stand up for herself. Not be just a victim.

She didn't know what was going to happen next, but she had a feeling that it was going to be such a challenge that she was going to need all of her strength in order to get through it.

Especially since she knew what she now wanted. She wanted to pursue her relationship with Isaac. She wanted to meet more girls and make more friends.

She wanted to live in peace. And that meant that she needed to be as strong as she could right now. If she was able to do that, the rewards would be worth all of the sacrifices.

After another moment in his arms, she pulled away.

He stared down at her in concern. "Better?"

She actually did feel better. She smiled. "*Jah.*"

"*Gut.*"

As they continued walking, they saw Ben, Jenny, Sam, and Freeman in the distance. They were walking toward the high school. Mr. and Mrs. Troyer were following behind them, chatting.

Freeman saw them first. Isaac's seven-year-old brother trotted toward them, a bright smile on his face. "What are ya doing walking this way, Isaac? The sandwiches are the other way."

Isaac chuckled. "I know they are. Hannah and I worked on them all morning. We'll be back there in a little while. We have an errand to run first."

Jenny must have seen something in Hannah's expression, because she walked up to her side. "What's going on?"

Though Hannah instinctively wanted to shield Ben and Jenny from the news, she knew that wasn't an option. Both of her siblings needed to be on their guard. "I saw Trent in the crowd at the high school. Isaac is going with me to tell the sheriff."

Jenny turned so pale, Hannah was worried that she might pass out. "Are you sure it was him?"

"Without a doubt. He's wearing a black ball cap and a yellow shirt and jeans. If you see him, stay far away."

Ben, who had overheard, had his hands fisted at his sides. "I'm tired of all of us dodging him."

"I am, too," agreed Hannah. "But I think there is a right way to deal with him, and that means asking the authorities for help. Until they catch Trent, I don't want you to get hurt." She looked up and noticed that Isaac was filling in his parents.

"We can go with ya," Mr. Troyer said.

"There's no need," responded Isaac. "We should be all right."

"Where are your parents, Hannah?" Mrs. Troyer asked. "Do they need anything?"

"I think they're still at home. I'll fill them in later."

"After we talk to the sheriff, we'll go to Hannah's house and talk to them. I think we're done with the big crowds today," Isaac said.

"We'll come over there as well," his father agreed.

Sam stared at him. "Daed, you're going to let us help out?"

"I think it's time we all started working together," Mr. Troyer said. "We like you, Hannah. We like you and Ben and Jenny, and we want to get to know your parents. That means we need to help you as much as possible." He paused, then added, "That means pushing ourselves a little out of our comfort zone—"

"I don't want you to get hurt," Hannah said quickly. "Trent's never done anything violent, but he might."

"If we all stand together, he won't stand a chance," Mr. Troyer said, his voice full of conviction. "It's only when we let our doubts get the best of us that problems occur."

Thinking back to all that had happened, Hannah had to agree. Keeping secrets and attempting to solve everything on her own hadn't worked out too well for her.

It was time she not only shared her secrets, but allowed others into her heart, too.

Chapter 23

Saturday, August 20

"I should have gone with them," Ben told Jenny as they continued their walk to the sandwich sale. "I should have insisted. Hannah should be with family right now."

"I thought the same thing, but there wasn't anything we could do, Ben," Jenny replied. "Besides, she seems pretty content with Isaac. She trusts him, too. She'd probably accept his help more than ours, anyway."

Ben nodded, though he looked a little disgruntled. "I guess you're right. No matter how old we get, she's only going to think of us as her little brother and sister."

"She kind of has a point," Jenny said. "It wasn't until recently that we did anything to make her think we could be of help to her."

Ben grimaced. "I feel bad about that. Don't you? I gave her the cold shoulder for months, blaming her for the move."

Jenny knew she'd acted far worse than that. Though it was tempting to simply agree, she felt compelled to be completely honest. "You might have given her the cold shoulder, but I was downright mean."

Ben winced. " 'Mean' might be overstating it."

"*Nee*. It isn't."

"Well, at least we've changed, yes?"

"We sure have, and for the better, too. You seem happier and I am, too."

"How do you think Mamm and Daed are doing?"

She barely refrained from rolling her eyes. "Who even knows? It's no wonder we're all so good at keeping our emotions to ourselves. They kept Daed's cancer from us!"

Ben looked haunted. "I don't like talking about Daed having cancer."

"I know." Though they'd lived their lives practically in each other's pockets, this was a situation where she wished she was a whole lot older than her brother. Then, maybe, she'd be able to force their parents to see reason and fight the cancer instead of simply accepting it without an argument.

As they walked on, Ben said, "Jenny, what if when Hannah goes home, Mamm and Daed don't take Trent being here seriously?"

She'd been wondering that, too. But someone had to look on the bright side. Since she was older, it had to be her. "I think they will. Mamm and Daed are learning that it's been a mistake to keep hiding with their heads in the sand."

"I hope and pray that they have."

"You and I will talk to them when we get home. And Mr. and Mrs. Troyer will, too."

Relief filled his eyes. "That will make a difference. Mamm and Daed will listen to them."

"I think so, too."

After another minute or two passed, Ben blurted, "They're great, aren't they?"

Jenny knew what he meant. The whole Troyer family was so open and forthright. It was refreshing after living the way the five of them had, keeping hurts and worries to themselves and always debating whether or not to share what they thought.

"Yeah," she agreed. "They really are."

Looking around the parking lot, Jenny noticed that it was still as crowded as ever. There were a lot of booths offering different things for sale, and a lot of families and groups of teenagers sitting on the soccer field eating sandwiches.

"Want to grab something to eat?"

"Sure. Mamm and Daed gave us money, we might as well use it," he joked.

When they got in line, Jenny looked around in case she saw someone she knew . . . as well as kept an eye out for Trent. The line was long and kind of plodding.

By the time they picked up their lunches, she was hot and more than ready to sit down in the shade. Or maybe even go home.

"Hey, Jenny," a voice said from behind her.

She turned abruptly. Then let out a sigh of relief. "Cole. Hi."

"I've been looking for you. When did you get here?"

"Just now. We decided to get our lunches first thing."

"Do you and Ben want to join us? I've actually already eaten one sandwich. I came up here to get another one."

Jenny turned to her brother. "Want to?"

"Yeah. Sure."

After they got their bagged lunches, they waited for Cole, then followed him to an area on the side of the school. There, about a dozen teenagers their age were sitting in the shade.

Feeling a little nervous, Jenny smiled at everyone. She had met most of them at church, but hadn't ever had the occasion to talk to them much, especially since she'd been so fixated on her hurt the first two months they were there.

Ben, on the other hand, was a lot more at ease. His joining the Amish school had been a great idea for him. It was obvious that he had been starting to make some good friends.

When he started to chat with them, Jenny and Cole were able to have a few minutes of privacy.

"How are you doing, really?" he asked.

"Really? Not too good," she replied, before almost instantly amending her answer. "My sister is having kind of a tough day."

"Want to talk about it?"

"Thank you, but I'd really rather think about anything other than Hannah's problems right now. Tell me about you."

Cole's brown eyes filled with humor. "Well . . . we had kind of a crazy morning. My older brother was here, working on this, so it was just me and my two younger brothers at home." He sighed, then blurted, "We broke a window."

"What?"

"Jasper and John decided to play catch in the front yard, and Jasper, well, he ain't too good of a ball player."

"How old is he?"

"Six."

It was almost hard to remember when she and Ben had been so young and getting into mischief. "So, he broke a window . . ."

"*Nee*, it was more of a group effort. John was tossing to him, Jasper was trying to catch . . . and I was attempting to teach them both."

"That was sweet of you."

"It was . . . but unfortunately, throwing and catching balls ain't my strong suit, neither. After a couple of tries, John threw the baseball just like I showed him, Jasper raised his hands to catch it just like I taught him, and the ball flew right into the front window." With a grunt, he said, "We really shouldn't have been tossing baseballs so close to the house."

"I'm thinking your parents weren't happy."

"You would be right. Mamm was not pleased," he said with a grin. "Neither was the cat, I have to say. The ball landed right close to where she was napping."

Jenny giggled. "At least it didn't hit your cat."

"John mentioned that, too. Anyway, after we cleaned up all the glass, found someone to replace it today, and weeded my mother's garden—our punishment for playing ball so close to the house —I came out here."

Jenny grinned. "That's the best story I've heard in ages."

"I hope not. Like I said, I'm pretty embarrassed about the whole thing. Most boys are better coordinated than me." He pushed up his glasses again. "And, of course, my brothers aren't going to keep it a secret—so before long, everyone is going to know what we did."

"It was just an accident, Cole. No one is going to think anything about it."

"You really mean that, don't you?"

"Of course I do. If you want to know the truth, I'm kind of surprised such a little thing upset you so much."

"Usually, it wouldn't. But, well, a man likes to think he can do most things other men can do, you know?"

She shook her head. "I don't understand that. Not really. But maybe it's because when I see you, I really just think about how smart you are. And nice. Those things count for a lot. At least they do to me."

Smiling at her, he unwrapped his sandwich at last. "Good to know."

Chapter 24

Saturday, August 20

Hannah's mother leaned back, her head against her kitchen chair, and sighed. "Oh, Hannah."

For the majority of her twenty years, Hannah had heard a dozen variations of the same sentiment. She'd heard *Oh, Hannah* when she'd lost the house keys. *Honestly, Hannah* when she'd gotten in trouble at school for talking too much.

Again, Hannah? when she'd accidentally burned cookies in the oven or when she broke the latch in their horse's stall.

Just as her mother often pressed her hands on Hannah's shoulders, rested her chin on the top of her *kapp*, and gave her encouragement, she uttered her name with a sigh whenever she didn't know what to do with her eldest daughter.

Oftentimes, Hannah didn't know whether to laugh or to cry when she heard her name spoken around a sigh. It seemed no matter how old she got, she found the familiarity of her mother's actions a comfort in a way.

As much as her world and situation changed, her mother's habits and reactions were steady and unchanging.

However, all she felt at the moment was hurt and irritation. After all, none of this was her fault. More importantly, she was standing up for herself. That was something to be proud of. "Mamm, Trent coming to Kentucky was not my fault. I did nothing to encourage this."

"I know that, child. But still, I thought we were going to get a reprieve at last." Before Hannah could point out that the arrival of the flowers and the note meant this latest occurrence was inevitable, her father intervened.

"May, after we got that envelope, we all knew it was just a matter of time before something else was going to happen."

Her mother looked surprised. "You thought that?"

"I did. It made sense to figure that Trent was going to show up sooner or later. I'm just glad that Hannah has Isaac here to help her."

Isaac, who had been sitting quietly while she'd shared the news, said, "I'm glad to help in any way I can. I want to help her, too. But I don't have the skills to make Trent stay far away from Hannah. That's why I think the sheriff's recommendations are so good."

Her father nodded. "*Jah*. Sheriff Brewer does sound like a good sort, indeed." Looking at

Hannah, he said, "I'm glad he is taking you so seriously."

"I am, too," she agreed.

Shifting in his chair, he added, "I think Sheriff Brewer made a good point about you always being with someone when you leave the house. I'm also glad he is actively looking for Trent right now, too. But I want to tell you that I've been doing some thinking and planning myself."

"What about?"

"I think it's time I stopped trying to do everything myself. I need help. *We* need help."

Her father was making this pronouncement as if he was the one who had gone to the sheriff's office that day. "I'm glad you feel that way, Daed."

"I'm going to help as much as I can," Isaac interjected. "My parents and siblings are, too."

"We are grateful for their help, to be sure. But something more needs to be done, I think." Sharing a look with her mother, her father said, "I think we need to ask the whole community for help."

Hannah blinked. "What do you mean?"

"Trent likes keeping you on edge. He is counting on you not wanting everyone to know about him. Let's ask everyone to help us catch him."

Before Hannah could respond, her mother stood up and walked to her father's side. "I think that's a fine idea," she said.

"You do?" Hannah felt kind of numb. Also a bit like she'd just stepped into another family's kitchen.

"*Jah*. You see, we made another big decision when we were at the doctor's office today."

Hannah watch her mother look over and smile at her father.

"We decided that Daed is going to begin chemotherapy."

"You changed your mind?"

"We did," her mother said.

"The Lord did the most amazing thing, Hannah," Daed added, turning more animated. "He put Phillip in my life today. You see, I met Phillip when I was first diagnosed in Millersburg. But while I elected not to fight the cancer, Phillip elected to go on chemotherapy immediately."

"We saw him today," her mother said, excitement in her voice. "Phillip was so happy, he was beaming."

"Beaming like he was helping the sun shine," Daed added with a nod. "He'd just received a CT scan and discovered that the treatment was working. Though nothing is guaranteed, of course, his doctors feel like he has turned the corner. He is going to survive."

"Can you follow his treatment?"

Daed shrugged. "I don't know. Phillip and me are very different people. He is English, I am Amish. He also has a different kind of cancer than

I do. There are different medicines for different types of disease, you see."

He lifted his chin. "But he has also had one thing that I have not, and that is hope. From the moment he was diagnosed, he only looked at this as a short period of inconvenience in his life. While I, well, while I decided that my life was near the end."

"You are going to fight." Tears filled Hannah's eyes as she contemplated what that meant to their family. "Father, this is the best news I've heard in ages. I'm so glad you aren't going to give up."

He nodded. "I'm ashamed that it took me seeing Phillip in the flesh to change my way of thinking. Here, I've been living my whole life coaching others to develop the strong faith that I had, when it seemed I was as much in need of tangible proof as anyone."

"You are being a bit hard on yourself," her mother said. "You were hoping for the Lord to heal you."

"I was. But I had kept my eyes blinded to all the evidence God had placed right in front of me. He gave me doctors and nurses who were trained to help me, medicine to help me fight my battle, and even a new friend to commiserate with."

Looking even more regretful, he continued. "But instead of being grateful for those gifts, I pushed them all away. It was as if I wanted to prove to Him that I was just as strong."

His words hit a chord with Hannah. "I think I was doing that very same thing, to some extent, with Trent." Looking at Isaac, she said, "When I first met Isaac, he called me the recluse. It really hurt my feelings. But now I realize that was what I had been doing. I had pushed away nearly everyone who could help me."

"And we weren't any help, either," Mamm said with a frown. "Instead of trying harder to fight Trent, we let him win." With a wince, she said, "We ran from Ohio, settled in here, and pretended that Trent's abuse couldn't have been fought. We somehow thought his treatment of you was something for us to be ashamed of."

Daed continued. "Instead of reaching out to others and asking for help, we ran. Furthermore, we let Jenny and Ben believe that you were the sole reason we moved when in fact we had our own private reasons, too. We let them blame you instead of opting to share our burden."

Hearing their confessions made tears well in Hannah's eyes. She'd never wanted to have Trent in her life again. But if one of the consequences of his reappearance was that her parents were finally becoming more open and honest, Hannah knew she should count that as a blessing.

Looking very tentative, her mother whispered, "I am so sorry for everything. Will you ever be able to forgive us, Hannah?"

"There isn't anything to forgive," she said

softly. "I love you and want you both in my life."

When her father held out a hand to clasp Hannah's, she took it gratefully. "Maybe we needed to start over here in Kentucky. For whatever reason, we all seem to have been refreshed."

Looking at Isaac fondly, her mother said, "Or maybe it's the company we've been keeping."

Hannah giggled when Isaac turned bright red. "Maybe so."

"For the record, I am not proud of the way I behaved," Isaac blurted. "I never should have called Hannah names. I have apologized for it. Several times."

Just as Hannah was about to explain that she'd brought it up to illustrate her mistakes, not highlight Isaac's, her father laughed.

"I doubt any of us knows what the future holds for us, Isaac, but if I may give you one piece of advice . . . ?"

"Of course," Isaac answered. "I'd be happy to hear it."

"Your female is always right."

Isaac blinked before his gaze warmed. "Always, Mr. Hilty?"

Sounding more at ease than he had in months, her father tilted his head back and laughed. "Oh, for sure and for certain. You see, once a man gets his head around that, the future is as good as gold." He winked. "It's a far sight more peaceful, too."

Chapter 25

Saturday, August 20

"I feel a little old-fashioned," Hannah admitted when she took a seat next to Isaac on her house's front porch swing. "We are much too old to be sitting here under my parents' watchful eyes." Feeling more than a little awkward, she added, "We can do something else, if you'd rather."

"I don't. I was just wondering if I should be thinking that we were much *too young* to be sitting here," Isaac replied. "My parents sit on our front porch all the time. My grandparents did, too.

That made her smile. "Perhaps front porch swings are good for people of any age."

He shrugged. "Well, at least courting couples." Laying out his arm along the back of the seat, he said, "Come a little closer, Hannah. If we're going to be sitting on this swing together, we might as well enjoy it."

She did as he asked, though to be fair, she was still wrapping her mind around the fact that they actually were a courting couple.

When had that happened?

When they'd first met, Isaac was a stranger she didn't trust. Later, he'd been the man who'd hurt her feelings by calling her names. Days after that, they'd become friends. Soon after, they'd become so much more than that. He was her protector, too.

But now? She supposed he was, indeed, her boyfriend. Or at least something very close to that. She knew what he meant to her. But what about him? "Isaac, have you done a lot of porch-swing courting?"

Isaac laughed. "Maybe once or twice."

"Don't leave me hanging like that! I want to hear about it."

"You do, do ya?" Using his foot to coax their swing into motion, he continued. "Well, let's see. The first time I sat like this was in sixth grade."

She almost choked on the iced tea she was sipping. "Sixth grade?"

"Uh-huh. I had a terrible crush on Rebecca, who sat behind me at school. I went over to her house to get some homework and ended up swinging by her side."

"You were a wily one, Isaac Troyer."

"Nah. Just determined."

She was enjoying the amusement in his eyes and the lighthearted conversation. "Did you put your arm up behind her, too?"

"Not at all! I actually didn't perfect that move until I was sitting beside Emilie."

"And that was when?"

"Fourteen."

She noticed that he didn't sound apologetic in the slightest. "Oh, brother," she teased. "I'm starting to see that I'm just one of many girls who have swung with you."

Leaning closer, Isaac wrapped the palm of his hand around the cusp of her shoulder. "That ain't true, Hannah. You are different, I promise. You just, well . . . you happen to be reaping the benefits of my youthful enthusiasm."

Hannah was about to tease him about how his hand was now resting on her shoulder, but she was afraid he'd move it if she did. Instead, she simply relaxed against him and enjoyed the moment.

She felt him inhale, then shift so he was holding her closer. Now much of her side rested against him. After a couple of more swings back and forth, she gave into temptation and rested her head on his arm.

It had been such a long day. First, the early morning sandwich making, followed by the Trent sighting, the sheriff's visit, and finally the illuminating conversation with her parents. She was exhausted and so glad that she had a shoulder to lean on.

"You doing okay?" he murmured after a few minutes had passed.

"*Jah*. I was just thinking about our day. It was a busy one."

"One of the hardest days ever," he said.

"Really? It was that way for you, too?"

"*Jah*. I hate that there is something bothering you that I can't fix."

"I think that's where you are wrong. Isaac, you took me to the sheriff and talked to Ben and Jenny, and also my parents. I'm grateful for that."

"Are you still afraid?"

"I don't think so." Then, considering it, she said, "I might feel afraid tomorrow. Maybe even later tonight. But right now, I only feel relaxed and happy."

"So I don't have to leave just yet?"

"Please don't."

"If you aren't ready for me to leave, then I won't." He ran a finger along her shoulder, playing with the fabric of her dress as much as anything. The simple, sweet movement relaxed her even further. And, because she completely trusted him, she closed her eyes and simply allowed herself to just be.

Now that the sun was setting, the temperature had cooled, and crickets were starting to chirp. Mockingbirds and orioles sang out, decorating the air with their joyful sounds.

The combination of Isaac's soothing presence, the lulling background noise, and the exhaustion from the day took its toll. The last thing she remembered thinking was that she should have probably encouraged Isaac to leave after all.

Isaac knew the moment Hannah fell asleep. One minute, she was snuggled beside him. The next, she'd been completely relaxed, her body a warm burden against his frame. He shifted slightly so he could support her better, wanting her to stay in his arms for as long as she or her parents would allow. He had a feeling if things were up to him, he'd stay that way for hours.

He'd been charmed by Hannah tonight. Until they'd sat out on this porch, he'd thought he'd already witnessed all of her moods. He thought he'd seen all she had to offer, but he realized very quickly that he couldn't have been more mistaken.

Tonight, he'd seen a fun and flirty side of her. A part of her that wasn't afraid. Maybe even a glimpse of the girl she'd been before a man had made it his goal to disturb everything she valued. What was funny to him was that he hadn't realized he had been missing this component. He'd thought she was perfect before.

A wave of protectiveness ran through him when she shifted. Instinctively, he moved to make her more comfortable. This was so different than how he'd felt when they were at the high school. Now he wasn't trying to protect her from danger. Instead, he was simply hoping to protect her happiness.

Which drew him up short. He had known he'd liked her very much. He had known he was drawn to her and wanted to make her happy. But tonight, for the first time, he realized why.

In spite of everything that had been going on around them, he'd been falling in love.

Chapter 26

Monday, August 22

Still worn out from the busy weekend, Hannah slept late on Monday morning. When she looked at the clock on her bedside table and learned that it was after nine, she leaned back on her pillows and sighed.

For the first time in months, she didn't wake up with a nagging fear in the back of her head. Her thoughts weren't filled with recriminations and self-doubts, feeling sure that she'd been losing her mind and simply imagining that she was being followed.

Gone, too, was the feeling of guilt that she'd been struggling with. She'd hated that she'd been the one responsible for dislocating her whole family. She knew now that Ben and Jenny no longer were mad at her and her parents had had their own reasons for moving to Kentucky.

Her optimistic feelings also stemmed from her time with Isaac this weekend. Never had she felt so content or relaxed with a man. She knew she was falling in love with him.

When she compared her optimistic feelings to all the dark moments she'd been experiencing, not even the knowledge that Trent was somewhere in Munfordville could damage her joy.

Because of all that, it not only felt like a new day, she felt as if she'd begun a new life.

She had just sat up in bed and begun to contemplate getting dressed when her door opened.

Jenny peeked inside, a cup of coffee in her hands. When she saw that Hannah was awake, her expression cleared. "Oh, good. You are finally awake."

"I am. I know I should feel badly about sleeping in, but I don't. Saturday was a big day."

"It was." Entering the room, she said, "Um, may we talk? I have something I need to tell you. I brought you coffee, too."

Her sister's expression was strained. Worried now, Hannah nodded. "Of course." Patting a spot on her bed, she said, "Come join me."

After carefully passing the mug, Jenny scrambled right up beside her.

"This reminds me of when you were a little girl," Hannah said after taking a fortifying sip. "Remember how you used to climb into bed with me in the mornings?"

"I do. I used to love that. You were much more fun than Mamm."

"I was just lazier." Hannah set her coffee cup down. "Now, what did you want to talk to me about?"

Right then and there, everything changed.

Jenny's expression tightened and she looked like she was about to get sick. "I did something bad, Hannah. I don't know if you'll ever forgive me."

Hannah was surprised. Hadn't they gone beyond this? "I will always forgive you, no matter what you do. Don't ever imagine that I wouldn't. You are my sister and I love you."

"You say that, but you don't know."

Hannah fought off smiling. Sometimes her sister was so dramatic! She supposed it was the age, but Hannah knew there was nothing that could shake her like the past few months had. "Just tell me, Jenny," she coaxed. "Waiting and worrying is always the worst. Just tell me whatever is on your mind. I promise, I will not get mad at you."

But instead of looking relieved, Jenny turned even paler.

"Jenny, now, if you will."

"Okay." After taking a deep breath, "I think I made friends with Trent."

"Trent Ritchie?"

Jenny nodded. "I . . . well . . . I think I'm the reason he found you again."

Hannah was certainly shocked, but she was even more certain that her little sister was very confused. "There is no reason you are to blame, Jenny," she said patiently. "Trent obviously did something to trace our path here. Maybe he got some information from the post office that had our forwarded address. Also, Kirsten told me that one of her letters to me had gone missing. I wouldn't be surprised if Trent had somehow stolen that note and got our address from the envelope."

Since Jenny still looked pensive, Hannah smiled at her reassuringly. "Do you see what I'm getting at, sister? If it was not one thing, it could have been another. It was not your doing."

"No, Hannah. You don't understand. I met Trent about two weeks after we moved here. I used to leave here and go meet him in secret."

Hannah set down her coffee cup. "You met him? Here?"

Looking miserable, her sister continued. "I promise, I didn't know it was your Trent. He told me his name was Shane. I thought he was just an older man who liked me."

Jenny's words rattled her, but Hannah was sure that she had simply gotten confused. "I find that hard to believe. After all, you knew what he looked like."

"I didn't. I swear, I didn't." Her voice turned more plaintive. "Don't you remember how you never met with him when the rest of us were around?"

"But you didn't think it was a strange coincidence that an Englisher was seeking you out?"

"Not really. After all, we've moved far away. And, plus, he really seemed to like me."

"But, still—"

"Hannah, why would you think I could feel any different than you?"

Hannah kept trying to find an excuse that made sense. "Maybe it wasn't actually Trent. Maybe you just think it might be, but it ain't."

"*Nee.* It was. I stopped talking to him when I realized that I shouldn't be secretly seeing a man who was so much older." Her voice cracked. "But by then, it was too late."

Hannah was really struggling to listen patiently and keep an open mind. "Too late. Why? What did you do?"

Jenny looked at her, then drew in a ragged breath. "I thought he liked me, Hannah. That's why I talked to him so much."

"What did you do?" Each word was uttered with force.

"I talked to him about you." Swiping her eyes with the side of her hand, Jenny hiccupped. "I thought he thought I was special, but he didn't. Not really. He was only using me to find out more information about you."

Every mixture of emotion that Hannah could fathom filled her. Hurt, confusion, anger, shock.

But overall, it was sympathy and, yes, empathy. She of all people knew what Trent was capable of. She also knew how charming he could be when he wanted something.

She understood how desperate Jenny had been

when they moved. Her little sister had been unhappy and struggling. Jenny had also had a lot of questions about what had actually happened between her and Trent, but Hannah had been so traumatized, she'd refused to even say his name.

"Jenny, please stop crying," she said quietly. "I understand. More importantly, I forgive you."

Abruptly, Jenny lifted her chin. Staring at her in surprise, she blurted, "You do? Do ya really?"

"I do. I told you that I love you." Though of course she always loved her sister, Hannah was amazed to realize that she really didn't harbor any anger toward her. They'd been through too much to hurt each other anymore.

"I love you, too," Jenny blurted as she flung herself into Hannah's arms.

Then she sobbed.

Holding her carefully, Hannah rubbed Jenny's back and did her best to hold her own tears at bay. She felt terrible that Jenny had been so afraid to tell her about Trent that she'd kept everything to herself.

She could only hope that when this was all over they'd somehow all learn to be open and honest with each other. Even if the truth hurt, it was always better in the end.

After another few minutes passed, Hannah sent Jenny out of her room so she could get dressed and wash up. Thirty minutes later, she found her father on the front porch in one of the rocking chairs. He had a thick folder in his lap and his reading glasses on.

She smiled at him as she carried the fresh cup of coffee she'd just made out with her. "How are you feeling?"

"About the same." Lifting the packet of papers, he said, "I've been trying to do some reading on all the treatments."

"It looks like a lot to take in."

"It is, but I asked for everything all at once. If I hadn't been so stubborn, I would have already learned a lot more about my illness."

"There is a time for everything, Daed. Maybe the Lord needed you to wait for some reason."

His expression eased. "That is a nice way to think of it."

"When do you go to the doctor again?"

"I'm going to the clinic this afternoon for some tests."

"I could go with you if Mamm can't."

"*Danke*, but Jenny and Ben are going to go with me."

Hannah was surprised. "Both of them?"

"They reminded me this morning that they are both getting older." Looking a bit amused, he added, "I think this is their way of proving that to me. I'm going to let them do that."

"I think that's a fine idea. Ben and Jenny have been showing me, too, that they can do far more than I realized. They are growing up."

"That they are, dear." He coughed. "Now, what about you today? Will you be okay if we leave you on your own for a bit?"

"I'll be just fine. I'm going to stay around here and get some housework done."

"You sure you will feel safe? I bet we could ask Mr. and Mrs. Troyer if one of them could come over and keep you company."

"That is not necessary. I'm stronger now, and wiser, too. I'll stay inside with the doors locked. I'm kind of looking forward to doing nothing more than cooking and cleaning."

Her father still looked uncertain. "You sure you'll be all right?"

"I'll be perfectly safe. Sheriff Brewer didn't say I needed a guard, just that I shouldn't go out and about by myself."

"Listen to him and don't take any chances. You can't be too careful until Trent is found," he warned.

"I intend to be very careful and very vigilant. I promise."

Her father sighed in relief. "I'm so glad every-thing is out in the open, daughter."

"Me, too. One day, God willing, we'll all look back on these days as special because it brought us closer together."

Holding out his hand, her father whispered, "Indeed, child. Even in the midst of darkness, there is always something to be thankful for."

• • •

Two hours later, Hannah was still thinking about her father's words. He had been so right. Even now, she had so many beautiful things to be grateful for. Each day was a gift.

Though she'd planned to stay inside, she eventually got tired of hiding in the dark. There was no way Trent was going to visit her at the house, anyway. Trent liked to watch her now, not speak to her.

After carrying her second load of laundry outside, she carefully shook out each item and started pinning them on the line. Then she made plans for the rest of her afternoon. It was a cherry pie kind of day, she decided. When she got back into the kitchen, she was going to sip iced tea and make a pie crust. Ben, especially, loved cherry pie. He'd be so excited to discover one cooling on the counter when he got back home.

Humming to herself, she tried to remember if they had any cream in the refrigerator. If so, maybe she could tackle ice cream, too. Few things were better than warm pie and homemade vanilla ice cream.

"You sound so happy, Hannah."

Startled, the gray dress Hannah was holding slipped from her fingers and fell to the ground. Then, her heart beating so quickly, she turned to face Trent.

He was standing only a few feet away. His arms

were crossed over his chest and he was wearing that black ball cap again.

Shocked that he could have arrived without her being aware of it, Hannah stared at him in shock.

He was staring at her, contempt in his expression. "What? Are you unable to speak now? You were so busy yesterday, talking to practically everyone in Hart County. Even the sheriff."

She hated how he sounded, so assured and full of scorn. "If you know all of that, you know that everyone is looking for you. You need to get off our property and go away, Trent."

He shook his head as he stepped forward. "That's not going to happen, Hannah. Not this time."

Only then did she realize that he had something in one of his hands. When she turned to run from him, he grabbed her easily.

And then she found out what he'd been clutching.

The shock of it made her cry out in pain, but there was no one around to hear.

Chapter 27

Monday, August 22

Isaac heard the clattering of footsteps before the door to his workshop opened.

Seeing it was Mr. Hilty, Ben, and Jenny, he raised a hand in greeting. But then their pensive expressions registered.

Alarm coursed through him. "What's happened?"

Mr. Hilty had come inside and was walking around the small workshop. Looking like he was attempting to peer into every nook and cranny, he said, "Please tell me that Hannah is here."

"She ain't." Feeling like his heart was in his throat, he choked out, "Are you saying that Hannah is missing?"

The older man nodded once. "I had an appointment at the clinic this afternoon. Ben and Jenny came with me. Hannah stayed at home by herself."

Though he, too, was starting to panic, Isaac attempted to be a voice of reason. "Perhaps she went for a walk or something?"

"She didn't," Jenny said. "The house was open and there was a basket of laundry in the yard."

"It looks like she was pinning clothes and then got sidetracked," Ben added.

"Plus, she promised me she wasn't going to leave the house," Mr. Hilty added. "Hannah wouldn't have left by herself. Not for any reason. She was afraid to do that."

Dread settled in the pit of his stomach. "Have you gone to the sheriff yet?"

"We went there before coming to talk to you," Hannah's father said. "Sheriff Brewer is concerned but thinks we shouldn't panic yet."

"Really?" Isaac didn't even try to hide his outrage. "After everything she's gone through?"

Ben jutted out his chin. "That's how I felt."

"When it was evident that the sheriff wasn't going to help us search for at least a couple more hours, we decided to come over here to you," Jenny explained. "It was a slim chance, but we started hoping that maybe she had decided to sit here while you worked. You know, to keep you company."

"*Nee.* I haven't seen her all day."

"I am afraid that Trent abducted her," Mr. Hilty said quietly. "I fear that he was tired of waiting. I canna think of any other reason for Hannah to be missing."

Looking him in the eye, Isaac nodded. "I'm afraid of the same thing. We need to get help."

"Will you help us?" Ben asked.

"Of course." Isaac only wished he felt more confident about his abilities to help. He was a woodworker. A farmer. Not a detective.

However, though he didn't know what might be the best course of action, Isaac realized he could only do his best. With that in mind, he started issuing directions. "Why don't y'all go on home? I guess Mrs. Hilty is on her way home already?"

Mr. Hilty nodded. "May is on her way there right this minute. She had to find a driver to take her home."

"Okay. While you go home and wait for Hannah, I'm going to talk to my parents and then visit a couple of people who put the sandwich auction together. They'll know the best way to get the word out about Hannah. One or more of us will then go over to your house and we'll hatch a plan."

Jenny's bottom lip trembled. "And if it turns out that she had just gone for a walk?"

At least he knew the right answer for that question! "Then we'll be glad about that. Don't worry about bothering people, Jenny. We are a community of friends. Every one of us is going to put the needs of our members first. I'm sure we'll start a prayer chain, too. That works wonders."

"*Danke. Jah*, we'll be praying, too. Prayer is mighty important, too." After shaking hands, Mr. Hilty walked back out, Ben and Jenny on his heels.

When he was alone, Isaac knew he needed to take his own advice. Gripping the edge of the workshop table, he closed his eyes and prayed.

More than ever, he needed to remember to stay positive and hopeful. He also needed to give up his needs to the Lord.

If there was anything he knew without a doubt, it was that he couldn't help Hannah alone.

"Please, God," he called out. "Please be with my Hannah now. Please be with us all."

The room was so dark that the faint band of light that peeked from under the door glowed like a bright flashlight.

Hannah didn't know how long she'd been on the floor of the dank basement, but she had a feeling that the light coming from under the door was from windows.

When night fell, that band would disappear and she would be enclosed in darkness. She shivered at the thought of her circumstances becoming even worse than they currently were.

From the moment she regained consciousness, Hannah attempted to take stock of her situation: She was sitting on a cold cement basement floor, leaning against a rough cement wall. Her hands were banded together with a rough rope and were in her lap. Her legs were stretched straight in front of her and her ankles were duct-taped together. Trent had taken great care to bind them tightly. Her bare feet were at odd angles with each other. The cramps that had been present in her legs had faded into an uncomfortable numbness hours ago.

She had no way to move, let alone attempt to get to safety.

The only blessing in the situation was that Trent hadn't covered her mouth or covered her eyes. After he'd bound her, he'd spent several long moments standing above her.

Then, he'd knelt and pulled off her *kapp* and let down her hair. She'd cringed when she'd felt his fingers glide against her scalp.

After that, he'd asked her if she loved him. When she said no, he'd yelled at her, then went out the door.

Hannah had heard his footsteps pound on the wooden steps leading upstairs. Soon after, she heard the faint slam of a door.

When she realized she was alone, she yelled for help. But she'd soon learned that no matter how much she cried out or yelled, no one was going to be able to hear her.

She was exhausted and scared of what Trent was going to do next. When he'd tased her in her yard, she remembered the severe pain she'd felt.

When she'd cried out and told him that she hated him, he'd tased her again.

Now she wondered what he was going to think of next to hurt her. "God, please help me," she whispered. "I am so alone down here. I am so frightened. Please give me strength. Please let someone find me, too."

As she heard his steps on the stairs, she braced herself for whatever was still to come.

When the door opened, Trent seemed surprised that she was still exactly where he'd left her.

She knew she needed to move. Her body hurt and there was no way anyone was going to be able to find her if she was stuck in the basement.

Desperate, she offered the best excuse she could think of. "I need to go to the bathroom," she blurted. Hoping to make her request even more believable, she forced herself to stare at him directly in the eye.

He focused on her, his eyes darting over her face, seeming to take in every red mark and tear stain. But he must have seen something else as well, because his eyes narrowed and his voice turned even more dark. "Do you think I'm going to fall for that?"

"What is there for you to fall for? It's the truth. I've been here for hours. You know what I say must be true." Actually, now that she'd brought up the subject, her bladder was letting her know that she'd had a real fine idea. "Let me go to the bathroom, Trent."

"Very well." Just as she sighed in relief, he grinned. "Let's play a game."

She didn't trust the new gleam in his eyes. "This ain't a game. I really need to go."

"I'll let you go on one condition. You need to

answer a question. If you answer me correctly, then I'll take you upstairs to the bathroom."

Trepidation touched every nerve. "Do you promise?"

Hurt filled his expression. "I don't break promises. You do. Don't ask me such things again, Hannah."

"All right. I—I won't."

"Good. That's real good." His eyes lit with expectation. "Now, are you ready to hear my question?"

Growing more troubled and frightened by the second, she nodded.

"Good girl. You are listening and obeying now." He kneeled down to one knee in front of her. So close that she could smell his expensive after-shave. "Now, here you go. Here is your question." He paused for a dramatic moment, then whispered, "Hannah, do you love me now?"

That question was as perverted and twisted as the way he had tied her up in this empty, dark basement. It made her physically ill.

So much so, that as much as she ached to lie in order to gain some freedom, she couldn't say such a thing to him. "*Nee.*"

Anger lit his eyes. "Even now you are refusing me?"

"I cannot love a man who hurts me, Trent." Forcing herself to think of the future and not her words, she said, "If you free me and let me go to the bathroom, maybe we could talk about things."

"Talk? There's nothing to talk about, Hannah. I am keeping you safe right now. I am saving you."

"Saving me from what?"

"From him, of course. From that man who was touching you. Who had his arms around you."

Last night. She realized then that Trent had been watching her and Isaac on her front-porch swing. While she'd been listening to the crickets and enjoying the comfort of Isaac's embrace, Trent had been watching from the woods.

He got to his feet and started pacing. "How can you trust a man like that? Why would you choose a man like him over me?"

Hannah had no idea what was safe to say. She was sure that anything she said would only make him angry. Therefore, she merely stared at him.

But he didn't like that, either.

"Answer me, Hannah," he commanded, each word sounding urgent. "Why did you ignore me yet let him touch you? Hurt you?"

"He didn't hurt me. He has never hurt me. Only you have."

When he tased her again, she realized that she should have guessed that was coming.

As the sharp, stinging pain threatened to take her breath away, her vision began to blur.

At least now, she didn't care.

Chapter 28

Isaac now knew he'd lived a hopelessly naïve and judgmental life. Ever since his hospital stay, he'd prided himself on his positive attitude and his hopeful outlook. He'd even found himself counseling others from time to time, using his own personal trials as his testament for his faith.

Now he realized that the Lord simply hadn't tested him before. Not really. Though he'd been in physical danger, he had also been extremely ill. He hadn't prayed and cried and suffered through his recovery, his parents had. He'd merely reaped the benefits of the doctors and nurses at the hospital.

As he waited for his father to join him so they could begin their search through the woods, Isaac leaned his head back against the outside wall of his house.

"Lord, I know I am weak, but I need you now," he whispered. "I have been prideful and selfish, using my life as a basis for others to admire. I realize now that that couldn't have been more wrong. It is not me who is worthy, but the person who has suffered alone in the shadows. I realize that now."

Opening his eyes, he looked into the sky. "Please be with Hannah now. I don't know what she is going through, but I do know she has to be scared. Please be with her. She needs to know that she's not alone. She needs to know that we all are going to find her. No matter what it takes."

He closed his eyes and offered his humble thanks then.

When the back door to their house opened and he saw his father, Isaac straightened at last. "You ready, Daed?"

"I am. I'm sorry I took so long." He pulled out a flashlight from the jacket he was now wearing. "I was looking for my best flashlight. I thought it might come in handy." Out of another pocket, he showed Isaac that he'd also grabbed a couple of water bottles and what looked like ten or twelve cookies in a zip-lock bag. "I thought some water and snacks would be good, too. If we find Hannah, she might be thirsty. And if we don't, well, we might be hungry and thirsty."

"I should have thought of those things. I don't have anything to offer but myself."

"Yourself is good enough, son," he said as they started to walk. "You looked mighty serious when I walked through the door. What were you doing out here?"

"Praying."

"I am glad to hear that." Gazing out toward the woods, he said, "I imagine Heaven is fairly ringing today with the sound of all of our prayers."

"I hope so. I asked the Lord to be with Hannah and give her hope and strength, Daed."

"From what you've told me, I have a feeling she is trying real hard to summon both of those things right now. I am sure our Lord is helping her as well. He is a good and powerful God."

As they entered the brush and wound their way through some overgrown rosebushes to the faint path, Isaac said, "Daed, do you think she's going to be all right?"

"I don't know. This man who has been liking her for so long seems like he's a bit hurt in the head. He might not be thinking straight."

They slowed their pace, looking for footsteps, particles of Hannah's blue dress, signs of a struggle, any of the things that the sheriff and his deputies had mentioned might be clues. "I feel a bit unworthy right now, Father," he whispered.

"Because you only have a willing heart but not a lot of detective skills?"

"*Jah*. It's like you read my mind."

"It's more like I've been thinking some of those same exact things." Stopping for a moment, his father rubbed a tree branch carefully before speaking. "I'm only a farmer, Isaac. I have experience running a farm and raising a family. This is out of my comfort zone. It makes me afraid I'm going to miss something that is important."

His father's admission surprised him. From the moment Isaac had told him about the Hiltys' visit, he'd acted so calm and assured. "But you were one of the first men to volunteer."

"Of course I was. The Hilty family asked for help and this girl is our neighbor. And, I think, possibly a person who is going to be important to my son."

"She already is. I think I'm falling in love with her." He cleared his throat, realizing that as hard as it was to do, he needed to talk about his newfound love for Hannah and his fears that he was failing her.

"Have you told her that?"

"I did. Well, I almost did the other night. I think she got the impression." As they stopped to look at a broken branch, Isaac said, "I hope she did. If I had known we might not have all the time in the world, I would have told her more directly."

"The Lord keeps giving us signs, doesn't he? With each sunrise, he shows us that each day is a beautiful gift. But sometimes I fear I only look at that sunrise as another day of work or obstacles."

"I'm guilty of that, too."

"What do you think of this broken branch, son?"

Isaac knelt by his father. Noticed that the twig was up high and it looked like it had been freshly broken. "I think it might be worth noticing, Daed. That definitely didn't happen on its own."

"Let's take a leap and imagine that Hannah or

that Trent character did this. What does that mean?"

Isaac looked around. Then, to his amazement, he saw the faint outline of a man's heavy work boot. "It means they went this way."

Smiling just then, his father said, "I think we might be heading in the right direction, son. Imagine that."

Isaac smiled back at him as they continued on. The brush and weeds and chiggers didn't bother him as much anymore. Instead, he was focusing with a new awareness at everything around him. With each step, he became more certain that they were on the right track.

And with that feeling grew something else. Doubts began to fade as hope filled his soul. Maybe they wouldn't be too late. Maybe they could make a difference. It was obvious to him that the Lord had answered his prayers.

If He had answered theirs, chances were better than good that He was listening to Hannah's prayers, too.

Isaac just had to hope that she was praying with all her might. *Don't give up, Hannah,* he shouted silently. *Hold on a little bit longer.*

Surely she could do that?

He hoped and prayed that was the case.

She'd been right. Now that daylight was fading, the thin line of illumination had vanished. Hannah was now sitting in complete darkness.

After she practically passed out from being tased again, Trent treated her even more harshly. He yelled at her, even slapped her when he thought she was looking at him in a disrespectful manner.

But when she pointed out that if she had an accident on his floor, he was going to have to deal with the consequences as much as she was, he cut off the tape bindings and led her up the stairs.

Each step had been painful. Her nerves were hurting and sent sharp signals up her legs each time she climbed a step.

But miraculously, Hannah hadn't had that accident and made it to the bathroom in time. Though he'd stood outside the door so she could have a tiny amount of privacy, he hadn't allowed her to shut the door. That meant that she didn't have any time to look around the bathroom or try to find any type of tool to help her escape.

Refusing her request for a sip of water, he roughly led her back down the steps, forced her back to the ground, and then taped her ankles together again.

"Do you promise to be good now?" he asked.

"*Jah.*"

"Speak to me in English."

"Yes," she whispered, though even saying that one word was painful. "I promise."

"Better. Now, you listen to me. You are going to

sit here and not move around. If you do, I'm going to either gag you or blindfold you."

"Don't do that." Her response couldn't be helped.

"What did you say to me?"

"Trent, please don't. If you gag me, I won't be able to breathe, and if you blindfold me, I will be terrified." Even worse than I am already.

"How badly do you want me to listen to you, Hannah?" Bending forward, he said, "Do you want to play our game again?"

She didn't want to. Of course she didn't. But she was too afraid of the consequences to do anything to upset him.

"Okay."

"What was that?" he barked. "Speak up when you answer me."

It was a struggle, but she uttered the words he needed to hear. "I mean, yes, Trent. I do."

"That's better." He kneeled on one knee again. "Hannah, do you love me now?"

"*Jah*." she said weakly.

"In English, Hannah!"

"Yes," she blurted. "I do."

He slammed his hand on the wall. "You do what?"

"I do love you, Trent."

His eyes glowed with happiness. Then, little by little, his expression changed to hurt and distrust. "You are lying."

"I am not," she lied. "I am telling the truth."

After staring at her for over a minute, his

expression turned completely contemptuous. "You haven't learned a thing, have you? No matter how patient I am with you, you are determined to fight me."

"I'm not," she cried, feeling frantic. "I promise, I love you." Every nerve in her body felt frayed and on the verge of stinging her.

But her plaintive cry didn't seem to affect him in the slightest. Instead, his face was an expressionless mask. "I am so disappointed in you," he uttered in a voice that matched his empty expression. Pulling out a rag from his jean pocket, he said, "What do you want, Hannah? To be blindfolded or gagged?"

Did she want to be blinded or silenced? No choice had ever been so hard.

So was the realization that he'd been actually playing another game with her. He'd come to the basement in order to hurt her further. It didn't matter what she'd say, he would find a way to either gag or blindfold her.

Even though Hannah knew she would likely regret this last bit of defiance, she kept her eyes averted and tried not to make a single sound.

All she could do was pray and hope that God hadn't forgotten her.

Chapter 29

Holding up the stack of flyers in her hands, Jenny turned to Cole. "Ready to tackle another street?"

"I am if you are," he replied in that positive, upbeat way of his.

"I think I am." She smiled hesitantly, not even sure if she was supposed to be even trying to smile. Was it wrong to be smiling if your older sister was likely being taken hostage by a man who had been scaring her for months and months? She was pretty sure it was.

And there came the tears again. She turned around and pressed her palms to her face in a futile effort to regain some of her composure.

Though lots of police officers were around the area now, many of the community had asked to help. When Sheriff Brewer ended up making copies of one of the photos that Trent had made of Hannah and then making flyers for people to distribute around Munfordville, Jenny volunteered to go with Cole.

Her volunteering had taken a lot of people off guard. Her parents were at home in the company of a police officer, fretting and holding out hope that Hannah was going to suddenly appear back at home.

Ben was with Sam Troyer and his parents. She wasn't sure if he was merely watching the clock and praying or trying to help, too. All she had known was that worrying and guilt were going to overtake her if she simply sat and waited.

That was why she had asked to help distribute flyers. However, it seemed it was just as difficult to hold her composure while being busy as it was when doing nothing.

"Hey," Cole said, lightly touching her arm.

"I'm sorry. I don't know what I'm doing."

"You probably shouldn't be doing anything. You need to rest, not be running around the streets of Munfordville. I should have told Sheriff Brewer that I'd go with someone else."

"I volunteered." Swiping her eyes again, she exhaled raggedly. "I just can't help but worrying."

"Of course you are upset. Anyone would be." To her surprise, he rubbed her back.

His touch, that reminder that she wasn't alone and that she had someone who cared about her, was what she needed to ask the question that had been tumbling around in her head for the last hour. "Hey, Cole?"

"Hmm?"

"Do you think she's still alive?" She kept her head averted. She didn't want him to see how desperate she felt—or how hopeless she was becoming.

He inhaled sharply. "Of course she is."

"We don't know that, though."

"You're right, we don't. But we need to believe that she is, Jenny. Don't allow yourself to think otherwise. I'm trying not to, but this is so scary. And he never did something like this before."

She could practically feel him weighing his different responses. Then he said, "Jenny, you need to have faith."

"I'm trying, but we don't know—"

"Stop," he commanded, his voice harsher than she'd ever heard it. "That's what faith is, yes? Faith is believing when you don't have proof. Faith is understanding that you can't control everything and that is just as well."

"I have faith in the Lord, of course."

"If you do, then have faith that He has not forgotten about Hannah."

"You are right. I'm sorry." Turning to face him again, she said, "My mind is so scattered."

"Stop apologizing. If you didn't care, you wouldn't be so upset." Holding out his hand, he said, "Come on. I'm going to walk you home now. You need to rest."

"Please, no. I'll get better."

"You are being too hard on yourself. Of course you don't need to act better. All you need to do is hope and pray. There are plenty of people in the community who will do all the hard work."

"I need to be doing something, too." She inhaled deeply. "I'm better now."

He looked doubtful. "Sure about that?"

"Very sure. Let's go." She held out her hand. "Do you mind if I still hold your hand for a little bit even if we aren't going home?"

He rolled his eyes, as if she'd just asked the silliest question ever. "Not at all."

Smiling at him again, they continued walking up driveways and knocking on doors.

Each person who answered couldn't have been kinder. Some had already heard about Hannah. Other people who hadn't heard at first were surprised, then concerned, then took the flyer and asked how they could help.

After they finished the street, they walked to the last street on the block. It was a quiet cul-de-sac, composed of only five houses, two of which were empty. One looked abandoned, another had a tilting for-sale sign in the front yard.

Cole held up their much smaller stack of flyers. "We're almost done. After this street, let's go back to your house and check in."

"Okay. That sounds like a good idea."

Looking like he was glad she had finally agreed to rest, he said, "I think it's my turn to knock."

"I think so." She couldn't help but giggle. After the first couple of houses, Cole had decided that they should alternate being the talker and lead person. Privately, Jenny didn't think it mattered, since they always ended up standing side by side and explaining the situation together.

However, this game definitely helped make each visit feel a little fresh and new.

While Cole knocked, she looked around. The yard looked especially bad. It was full of weeds and looked parched. Nothing looked like it had been taken care of.

Though it was obvious an Englisher lived there, she figured they must either have fallen on hard times or were trying to conserve their money. One of the windows was opened about halfway. Most Englishers would have their houses tightly closed and their air-conditioners on.

No one answered. Cole glanced at her. "I don't think anyone is here. We should probably just go."

"Knock again." Pointing to the open window, she said, "I don't think anyone would leave their house open like this."

Cole looked as if he didn't believe her, but he did as she bid and rapped on the door again. "Hello?" he called out.

Just then, they heard a clang and the click of a door closing.

Jenny smiled. "I was right. Someone is here."

"I wish they'd come to the door, then. It's getting kind of hot on this doorstep." Cole rapped his knuckles against the door again. This time, a little bit harder. "Hello?"

They heard the sound of footsteps and a grunt. Then, at long last, the sound of a deadbolt being turned.

"Finally," Cole said with a wink in her direction as the door opened. "Hiya," he said the moment he looked up at the man on the other side. "We're wondering if you've seen this woman."

Just as Jenny was about to move to Cole's side, she got a good look at who had appeared at the door.

Then her heart felt like it stopped as their eyes met.

"Cole, run!" she screamed as she skittered backward down the stoop. She could hardly think. All that made sense was that she needed to get away from there as fast as possible and get help.

Cole turned abruptly, his face a picture of confusion. "What? Jenny—"

"Go!" she interrupted. Then screamed as loudly as she possibly could. "It's him! It's Trent!"

Trent rushed out to grab her, but Jenny started running down the street as fast as she could. She didn't even stop to look to see if Cole was following her. She could only hope he was. If he wasn't, she knew she couldn't help him, and she really wasn't going to be any good to help Hannah by herself.

When she got to the end of the street, she screamed again. "Help!"

Less than two seconds later, she heard people answer her back.

"What's wrong?" a woman called out. "Where are you?"

Glancing up at the street sign, Jenny yelled, "I'm on Maple. He's here! Someone get the police!"

To her relief, she heard a burst of sirens just as everything converged at once. She heard more calls of support, saw two English men running her way, and then felt a heavy hand push her forward.

She landed hard on her hands and knees—closed her eyes and braced herself to be kicked or hit. When it came, it was almost a relief, because then she knew that she'd done something to help her sister.

At last, Hannah was safe from this man.

Trent started yelling profanities just as a police car pulled up and some Englishers tackled him.

Jenny closed her eyes and prayed that she and Cole hadn't been too late.

Chapter 30

Monday, August 22

It is a blessing to be able to see, Hannah continually told herself in the dark basement. It is a blessing to be able to see.

Those words had become her mantra from the moment Trent had stuffed a dirty rag in her mouth and left her shaking on the basement floor.

Counting her blessings had never been so important to her very survival. Hannah felt as if she had nothing left but her faith and the ability to look for something to focus on that was positive. Instinctively, she realized that focusing on her fear or pain would only make her fall even further apart.

After Trent had stuffed that rag in her mouth, she'd gagged and almost had a panic attack. Especially when Trent sat down across from her and started talking.

In a monotone voice, he'd told her about the future he planned for them. The way she would always be his. She would always be perfect because he would make her that way. He would make sure she always remained the way she was.

He told her how he'd rented this house and how it was on a small, run-down street in a forgotten area of town. How most of the houses were vacant.

How no one would ever guess who he was, or probably would even imagine that anyone lived in the house. How, as soon as she had grown biddable, he was going to take her far away from there. He was going to change her clothes and dye her hair.

In no time, she would look completely different and no one would ever imagine that she was Hannah Hilty.

She would only exist as his wife and mother of his children.

Every word he uttered made her feel sick inside.

She hated the way he spoke so sincerely, so matter-of-factly. As if every word he said was a fact that couldn't be disputed.

Because she was afraid he would blindfold her if she looked away, she'd taken care to stare at him directly in the eyes the entire time he said his long and involved speech.

After an hour or so, he had gone back upstairs.

Knowing she could do nothing else, she started praying and counting her blessings.

You can see, she reminded herself. God is with you and you can see.

She repeated those sweet phrases over and over. They also calmed her. Eventually, she was hardly aware of his footsteps above her.

But when she heard the sharp rap on the door, followed by the faint call, her heart raced.

A door slammed. Trent was obviously pretending he wasn't home. But whoever was there didn't give up. The knocking continued.

Moments later, Hannah heard Jenny scream.

Her palms began to sweat as all the consequences of that hit her hard. Especially when she heard the door slam and Jenny screaming for help.

Pulling against her bindings, Hannah sat up. Attempted to shift, maybe even find a way to push herself to the stairwell.

But of course, there was nothing she could do. Her bindings were too tight and her muscles had long since cramped up.

All she was capable of doing was waiting and imagining what Trent was doing to her little sister.

Tears slid down her face as she realized that something worse than her worst imaginings had occurred. Somehow, she had not only been responsible for her own captivity, but she was going to be responsible for Jenny getting hurt, too.

Helpless, she began to cry harder, blinking her eyes against the torrent of tears and nearly choking on the rag in the mouth.

Then she heard the front door slam open. She braced herself for Trent to come down the stairs with Jenny in his arms. Braced herself to accept that she was responsible for hurting her sister and that she was going to have to watch Trent hurt her.

"Hello? Hannah, are you here?"

She stilled, confused. That wasn't Trent.

After the space of a heartbeat, a voice said, "Hannah, this is Sheriff Brewer. It's over, Hannah. We have Trent in custody and he can't hurt you again. Now, can you help us find you? We want to help you, honey."

Tears filled her eyes. Help had come! She wasn't alone!

But of course, with the gag in her mouth, she couldn't answer.

"Hannah? Do you hear me? This is the sheriff, Hannah. Trent isn't here. You're safe."

Thinking about Jenny, thinking about Isaac,

about her family, she knew she had to do something.

"Hannah?!"

Using all her might, Hannah shifted her body to the side and tried to kick the wall with her bound feet. It took three tries, but at last she was able to make a sound.

"She's here," Sheriff yelled as he started directing people throughout the house.

"Hello?" another voice called out. "Hannah, can you answer us?"

God, please be with them. She silently cried out. Please help them.

Seconds later, the basement door was opened and a blinding light was turned on.

"Hannah?" Sheriff Brewer called out, taking one, then two steps at a time down.

Still struggling, Hannah attempted to make another noise. Anything so he wouldn't turn around and close the door again. She kicked the wall weakly one more time.

Then he spied her. "Heaven help us," he murmured before rushing toward her. "Down here," he yelled as he got to his knees and wrapped an arm around her back as his other hand gently pulled out the gag.

She inhaled deeply as she cried harder.

Then gasped when she realized that Isaac was one of the men who had arrived.

"Isaac?" she rasped.

"You're here," he said, his voice tight with emotion. Kneeling down, he carefully gathered her into his arms after Sheriff Brewer pulled out a sharp knife and cut through her rope and duct-tape bindings. "Oh, Hannah. I've been so worried about you."

"It really is you, isn't it, Isaac?" she said around a hiccup. She still felt as if she was in the middle of a dream.

"It is," he said, running a hand along her loose hair. "I've been so worried. So worried."

His words were comforting. His kind, loving tone even more so. Collapsing against Isaac's shoulder, she inhaled, taking comfort in his fresh, clean scent and the way his strong arms were holding her close, making her feel whole again.

After he held her for another minute or so, Hannah reluctantly pulled away. A roomful of people surrounded them, no doubt waiting to ask her questions. She also had just realized that she hadn't spied her sister in the crowd. Was she hurt?

Bracing herself to hear the news, Hannah turned to the sheriff. "Sheriff Brewer, what about my sister, Jenny?" she asked. "I am certain that I heard her scream. Is she all right?"

Sheriff Brewer beamed. Positively beamed. "Your Jenny is a little bruised and banged up, but she is okay. She's our hero, Hannah."

The words didn't quite register. "Hero?" she

whispered. "Are you saying . . . saying that she's okay?"

"She is. I promise," Sheriff Brewer said.

Isaac slipped his hand into hers. "That's *gut* news. Ain't so?"

Before Hannah could reply, another man knelt down beside her.

"Hannah, I'm Frank Burns," he said in a kind voice. "I'm the owner of A&L Grocery. I know Jenny pretty well. I just want you to know that I saw the EMTs help your sister and her friend Cole myself. Jenny is a little bruised and battered, but she is going to be just fine." Smiling encouragingly, he said, "Why, she was talking to everyone. And, of course, more concerned about you than herself."

"And what about Cole?"

"He's got a good bump on his head, but he is going to be all right as well."

"I hope he is. I've been so worried."

The sheriff chuckled. "Hannah, you are the one who has been in all of our hearts and minds. We've all been worried about you. Now that you are found, it's all going to be okay. I promise."

Above them, Hannah heard more footsteps and radios. "Down here!" Sheriff Brewer called.

"We've got the ambulance in the driveway and a car out to her parents' house," a uniformed man said as two medical personnel carrying a stretcher started down the stairs.

Behind them, more police officers arrived, some taking pictures of the area. The noise and the flashing of cameras and the radios screeching at each other were disconcerting, but Hannah didn't care. She was simply too relieved that her nightmare was over.

Sheriff Brewer knelt by her and held her hand. "We're going to get you out of here and get you to the hospital, but first I need my team to take a couple pictures. I know you don't like your picture taken, but could you make an exception for me? We need these photos for evidence. We have to make sure Trent goes to jail for a very long time."

"We have to do whatever we can to help them, Hannah," Isaac said.

"I agree. If taking my picture here will help, please take it."

"But quickly, *jah*?" Isaac said as he stepped away to let the investigative team have the space they needed.

"We're going to get this done as fast as we can," Sheriff Brewer promised. "I, too, want to make sure your girl gets out of this place as soon as possible."

His girl? Hannah looked over at Isaac just as several cameras began to click.

Everything around her became a blur as medics helped her get on the stretcher, then poked and prodded her.

The last thing she was conscious of thinking before they loaded her into the ambulance was of how glorious it looked outside. The sky was blue. It was warm. The air was fragrant with the scent of grass and the nearby woods.

She could see it all. Feel it all.

She was free.

She was blessed.

Chapter 31

Two days later
Wednesday, August 24

"Hannah, I'm starting to wonder if you're ever going to eat a meal at the kitchen table again," her father teased as he stepped out on the front porch with a grilled cheese sandwich on a plate in one hand and a tall glass of lemonade in the other.

"I can't help it. I love the fresh air. I'd sleep out here on this porch swing if I could." Actually, Hannah thought it was going to be many, many weeks until she could be anywhere that reminded her of being confined in a dank, dark basement. Only the warm breeze and sights and sounds of the world around her seemed to ease her worries and aches.

Well, that and Isaac.

"You hearing this, Isaac?" her father groused with a wink.

Sitting in a chair he'd pulled up beside her, Isaac chuckled. "I am. I guess, one day soon, I'm going to have to help add a screen to the porch so the bugs don't get to her in the middle of the night."

Taking a bite of her sandwich, she said, "*Danke* for the sandwich, Daed. It tastes *gut*. *Wunderbaar*."

"I'm glad. I just made one for myself." Looking a little chagrined, he said, "I decided to eat as many as I can this week since my chemotherapy begins next week."

"That's a good plan."

With his hand on the door, he paused. "You going to be okay out here with this boy?"

"I'll be fine." She was going to be better than fine, she knew. Every time she thought about those endless hours spent on the basement floor of Trent's house, she knew she'd never take anything for granted again.

After the policemen had taken pictures, the EMTs had loaded her onto a stretcher and whisked her upstairs and into an ambulance.

When she arrived at the hospital, she'd been asked even more questions and her wrists and ankles had been cleaned and bandaged.

By that time, her parents had picked up Jenny and Ben and made their way to the hospital, too. Her mother cried when she saw Hannah's bruises and cuts. Her father looked as if he was on the verge of tears as well.

But they were all okay.

After they'd been home a couple of hours, Jenny climbed into bed with her and they held each other and cried. Both of them had been in so much danger. It was a true blessing that no one, not even Cole, had been hurt worse.

Hannah was recuperating ever since, deciding after a while to spend as much time outside as she could.

Bringing her back to the present, sitting on the front porch, she heard Isaac call her name.

"*Jah*?" she asked.

Looking bemused, Isaac got to his feet, then moved and leaned against the porch railing so they were directly across from each other. "Your father's right, you know. I do need to make sure you have someplace safe for you sit out at night."

She shrugged. A couple of mosquito bites were never going to be a big issue for her ever again. Also, well, he had already done so much for her. How could she possibly ask him for more? "That's sweet of you to say, but it's not your problem."

"I might think differently."

She looked at Isaac, aching to ask what, exactly, he meant. Then she felt that same awkwardness that she'd experienced when they'd first met. How should she act? She wasn't exactly sure.

She didn't want to push him into doing anything he wasn't ready for. Even more importantly, to her at least, she didn't want to misinterpret his words. That would embarrass them both.

She made do with sidestepping their conversation. She stretched out her legs and arms, relishing her freedom of movement. "Sometimes I can't believe we are talking about things like mosquitoes and grilled cheese sandwiches. When I was sitting on that basement floor, I thought I'd never care about anything so mundane ever again."

He moved his hat back so she could see his expression better. "Bugs and comfort food aren't mundane things, though."

She raised her eyebrows. "You don't believe so?"

"Nope." Pushing off from the railing, he moved to sit down next to her. "I think a good life is made up of hundreds of things like that."

She understood what he meant. "You know, I think you're right. It's the small things that count."

"It is. Life is made up of hugs and smiles, tears, and disappointment. Of ice cream and grilled cheese and pesky bugs and rays of sunshine."

She liked his list but knew he'd forgotten something important. "And friends and family, too."

His eyes lit up, obviously liking her addition. "*Jah*. And those things, too. Each day the sun rises, lifts above the sky, and sets again. It's glorious and perfect. Just like all those things we mentioned. It's all to be savored. Life is to be savored."

Thinking about their last couple of weeks, she smiled slightly. "*Jah*, I think you are right. Each day is a blessing. Sometimes days pass in fits and starts, but time does move on. Always."

"I'm so glad you are going to be all right and that Trent is in jail."

"Me, too. Sheriff Brewer thinks he's going to go away for a very long time. I'm free of him. At last."

Unable to help herself, she stretched her arms out in front of her, moving her hands this way and that.

Isaac caught one hand, then the other. Studying them, and her wrists, which were still slightly bruised, he said, "Do your arms and legs still hurt?"

"*Jah*. Well, they ache. The *doctah* said that they would for a while."

He ran a finger along the fine bones of her wrist. "He had you so tightly bound, it's a wonder he didn't cause more damage."

"I know." She didn't want to talk much more about it. The doctors and nurses had asked all kinds of questions when they examined her. They'd also mentioned the many things that could have resulted from her tight bindings but hadn't.

When Isaac wrapped an arm around her and

then pulled her close enough for her to rest her head on his chest, Hannah allowed herself to rest against him. Just like she had the evening before Trent had abducted her.

They rocked for a while. With her body snugly nestled against his and the warm air soothing her skin, Hannah allowed her mind to rest. She didn't want to think about anything other than how good it felt to be in Isaac's warm embrace. She heard Isaac's heart beating steadily against her cheek. The steady beat comforted her as much as the feeling of security she was feeling.

Just as her eyes were drifting closed, Isaac shifted and cleared his throat.

His actions caused her to sit up so she could look at his face. He looked a little nervous.

"Isaac, what's the matter?"

"How sore are your legs?"

"They are stiff but okay. Why?"

"I'd like you to go on a walk with me. If you can handle it, that is."

"Um, I can handle it, if it ain't too far."

"It's not. Maybe a fifteen-minute walk."

She got to her feet. "Let me go tell my parents and I'll be right out."

When she joined him again, he held out his elbow and she grasped it, enjoying the old-fashioned, courtly gesture.

To her surprise, he took her the opposite way of his house. They stayed on the main road but took the first right turn, entering the middle of a street filled with older houses on half-acre lots. "Have you been down this street before?"

"*Nee*. I never had an occasion to walk here." Of course, until, well, today, she hadn't felt comfortable walking anywhere. She looked around. Several yards had Amish children playing in them. There were also a couple of Englishers.

Everyone looked like they were doing what she and Isaac were doing. Enjoying the cooler evening air.

"Is there any special reason we are walking this way?" Perhaps there were more of his friends he was ready to introduce her to?

"Actually, there is," he said as they continued to walk.

Isaac touched the brim of his straw hat to an older couple sitting on their porch swing, just the way she and he had been a little while ago.

"I am trying to find a way to tell you that I did something yesterday." Looking a little frustrated, he continued. "Unfortunately, I can't think of an easy way to say the words."

"In an easy way, hmm? If there's something you want to discuss, I think you should just say it."

But instead of looking relieved, he looked even more agitated. "I don't think it's as easy as that."

"It might be. I promise, I'm stronger than I look."

"I know you are strong. Believe me, I won't

ever think of you as anything other than strong again."

Hannah appreciated his sentiment, but she was sure that there was something else he wanted to discuss. "Tell me what's on your mind, Isaac," she said. "I promise, whatever it is, I can take it."

"I suppose you can," he mused as he drew them to a stop in front of a small white house with a long, winding driveway leading up to it. "So, I did something yesterday." He inhaled, shrugged, and finally said, "I put an offer on this house."

She gaped at him before turning to look at the place more closely. She noticed that there were a lot of trees on one side of it and a brick fireplace that someone had long ago painted white. It also had a porch that not only covered the front but one of the sides, too. All in all, it was a lovely house. Picturesque and charming. "Congratulations," she said. "It's very pretty."

"Would you like to see it better?"

"Of course."

Looking a little more at ease, Isaac escorted her through the front yard. She noticed the remains of a garden, the shed that was painted green and white but was in need of a new roof. Most of all, she liked how peaceful it was. It was in the middle of a street. With the trees and the big lot, one would feel at peace but not completely alone.

He pointed to the shed. "I'm going to rework that so I can one day have my workshop here."

She thought he was going to guide her up the front steps, but instead of doing that, he took her to the side that didn't have the porch.

"I bought this house for a lot of reasons, but mainly for this spot here."

"What's so special about it?"

"I'm going to build a wide, covered screened-in porch here."

For some reason, that made her sad. Maybe because it signified that he was very ready to move on.

To move on without her. Though her mouth felt dry, she did her best to say the right words. "That . . . I mean, that will be lovely."

"Do you really think so?"

"Of course."

He smiled. "Good. Because I bought it for you."

She gaped at him. "What?"

"I bought you a house yesterday. I want you to live here with me one day. When . . . when you think you will be ready. When you will be ready to be happy here."

That was an unusual way to phrase things. But she couldn't deny that he had a point. One had to be ready to be happy. It wasn't simply a state of being, it was a state of mind. "Are you proposing to me, Isaac?"

"I am. Well, kind of."

"Kind of? That tells me nothing."

"Hannah, I am going to work on this house. I am

going to put a swing on the front porch and a screened one on the side. Then, I want to spend lots of evenings sitting on that swing and wrap my arms around you."

His words were painting such a lovely picture, such a vivid one, she felt herself shiver. Not from fear, but from expectation. "Hmm."

He studied her, then obviously seeing that she wasn't shocked, he continued. "When I do all that, I'm going to tell you how I feel about you."

"You don't want to tell me such things now?"

"Not yet," he said, quietly blowing out a burst of air. "I want to share all those things when the time is right. When you are ready." Gazing at her closely, he added, "When I am ready. When *we* are ready."

Even in the dim early evening light, she could see that he was blushing. And, she reflected, she liked that idea. That there was time to wait for the right moment. That they didn't have to be in a hurry for anything because they had such a future to look ahead to together.

What could be more special than that?

"I'll look forward to that day, Isaac."

He exhaled. Smiled softly. "Me, too. We are going to have a good life, Hannah. A happy one. I am sure of it."

Standing there on a patch of dirt, beside a house that wasn't quite done, dreaming of a future next to a man who cared enough about her to wait for the timing to be right, Hannah nodded.

They were going to have a happy life. No matter what the Lord had in store for them. That much she was certain of. "I think so, too," she said, smiling at Isaac. Smiling at the world around her.

Smiling with her heart full of hope and free from secrets.

At last.

Meet Shelley Shepard Gray

In many ways, my writing journey has been like my faith journey. I entered into both with a lot of hope and a bit of nervousness. You see, I didn't get baptized until I was in my twenties and didn't first get published until I was in my thirties. Some people might consider those events to have happened a little late in life. However, I feel certain that God knew each took place at exactly the right time for me.

To be honest, these days I rarely stop to think about my life before I was a Christian or a writer. I simply wake up, drink my coffee, and try to get everything done that I can each day! I feel blessed to be a part of a large church family and to have a busy career. But, every so often, someone will ask why I write inspirational novels. Or why I write at all.

Then I remember how it felt to knock on a minister's office door and tell him that I wanted to be baptized. And how it felt the very first time I wrote "Chapter 1." Both felt exhilarating and nerve-wracking.

Perhaps you are a little bit like me. Maybe you, also, developed your faith a little after some of your friends or family. Maybe you, also, began a new job in a field that you didn't go to school for. Maybe you started on a journey where you weren't sure you were going to be successful or even fit in.

Or maybe, like me, success wasn't what you were hoping to attain. Maybe it was a matter of following a power bigger than yourself. If so, I'm glad I'm in good company. I'd love to know your story, too.

Now I have been a Christian for almost thirty years. I've been a published writer for about half that time. Both journeys have not always been easy. Both have been filled with ups and downs. Yet, both have given me much joy, too. I'd like to think that anything worth having takes some hard work. It takes some time to grow and mature, too.

And because of that, I am comfortable with the fact that I'm still on my journey, one morning at a time.

With blessings to you,
Shelley Shepard Gray

Dear Reader,

Thank you for joining me in Hart County! This series has been a rather rejuvenating experience for me. It meant working with a new agent and a new editor. It meant pushing myself a little bit, even after writing thirty-five Amish romances. Now, as I write this letter, I realize I couldn't be more excited about this series or this book in particular. Change, I think, can be a very good thing.

The Amish of Hart County series will be a little different than most of the other series I've written for Avon Inspire. Though each book will be loosely connected and set in Hart County, Kentucky, each novel will be written as a stand-alone novel. This allows me to make this series a little longer than my previous ones. There will be six books in this series, being released over the course of two years.

This series will also be suspenseful in nature, too. Though each book is a romance, it will have a slightly different slant than some of my other novels, which centered on mainly family dynamics. Again, it's been a nice stretch for me as a writer.

I hope you enjoyed the book! I loved traveling to the middle of Kentucky and spending a couple of days exploring the area. I loved visiting with the Amish in stores and sitting next to a group of them in a Mexican restaurant. I enjoyed Kentucky's rolling hills and winding roads, those deep, lilting Kentucky accents, and the dry wit that so many folks in the area have. I loved seeing the horses and the blue grass and the wide open skies and the houses and buildings made out of limestone. Hart County, Kentucky is someplace new for me. It's filled with new possibilities and a wealth of opportunities.

I hope you'll come along for the ride.

With blessings to you,
Shelley

Q & A with the Amish

One of the reasons I enjoy writing novels featuring the Amish is because I live in Ohio near several Amish communities. One community is just an hour from my house! Because of this, I've had the opportunity to visit different Amish communities several times a year, both in Ohio and Kentucky.

Over time, I've been blessed to know several Amish ladies well enough to call them friends. Because of this friendship, they were kind enough to let me interview them about everything from faith to canning to learning to drive a buggy. I hope you'll respect their privacy and understand that I won't be using their names, only their initials. I also am not listing the community where they live.

Enjoy the interview! Even after all these years, I learned something new!

Shelley: What were some of your favorite childhood activities? Are they different from generation to generation?

B: Yes, I'm sure they are different from generation to generation. We liked to play croquet in the summer. Nowadays, it's a lot of volleyball. We also played a lot of board games and cards, like Uno, Rook, and Phase 10.

J: Growing up on the farm I always enjoyed outdoor work, being around the animals, helping with the garden, and putting in hay. Our family always had ponies and riding horses, which we enjoyed. I would say some things have stayed the same. Most Amish children have a pony during their growing-up years. Not very many families are doing farming anymore, so that has changed some things, but children help do yard work, help in the house, do dishes, etc. Of course, there are those few that are spoiled and don't do much to help.

Shelley: When did you learn to sew and quilt? Did you learn from your mother? Did your daughters enjoy sewing and quilting, too?

B: Yes, I learned to sew from my mom, but I didn't do much of it before I was married. It was easier to let my mother do the sewing and I do the other work, because I didn't really like it.

After I got married, I sewed. I also didn't like to quilt at first but really like it now. One daughter really liked to sew and quilt and the other one didn't like it; she liked working outside.

J: I was taught to sew as a teenager. I was left-handed so I kind of learned by myself as my mom was right-handed and it was hard. My daughters taught themselves and from watching me. They learned at an early age, and they like to sew lots more than I do. Quilting is not so much a hobby anymore; the young generation are not all taught to quilt.

Shelley: What about canning and gardening? What do you like to can? Has the process changed much over the years?

B: I like to can green beans, four different kinds of pickles, applesauce, and apple pie filling. We freeze the corn and peaches. We also can a lot of pizza and pasta sauce.

J: Our family has always done a lot of canning and gardening. I enjoy it very much. I like to can most anything. I do my own sauerkraut. We also grow a lot of popcorn. My garden is always bigger than most other people's. There are Amish people who do not have a garden and will just buy at produce stands, etc. For me, gardening is relaxing and is very much a stress reliever.

Shelley: How does your faith guide your life?

B: By reading the Bible and praying. Also attending church.

Shelley: Driving a horse and buggy looks hard to me. Was it difficult to learn to do that?

B: Usually, we learn with a tame horse. Some horses don't like big trucks. They sometimes jump towards the ditch. You have to have the lines tight, then they can't do too much.

Shelley: Do you have favorite recipes that you like to make for other people?

B: Yes, I make coffee cake for coffee breaks with friends. I also like to try new recipes.

Shelley: Has your community changed much over the years?

J: Our community has changed a lot, with hardly any farmers left. Most people live on smaller properties, anywhere from one acre up to ten acres. Some have more land and will do some hay crops. Along with no farms, people have more time for leisure activities and will spend time camping, spend evenings around campfires with friends, go out to eat, and spend more time with family, etc. As times change, rules change. We have generator power for washers, sweeper fans, sewing machines, etc. Also solar power for some.

We also have a lot more youth gatherings, volleyball, and singings. Most people are accepting of changes. There are always a few that hang on to the old ways.

Shelley: What was Amish school like?

J: For me, going to school in the 1970s and 1980s, we always talked Amish during school. Then in the seventh grade we got a new teacher and everyone had to talk English. Wow, that was hard! We knew enough English to get by before that, but I suppose we probably did not always use the proper words.

Now all children must speak English at all times during school. Now most children know English even before school, as people have more contact with the English and often have friends they get together with. Our children went to public school with approximately twenty-five to thirty other Amish in their grade when starting kindergarten. As time went on and more Amish schools were built, some would drop out of public and go to Amish school. Also, a few do homeschool.

I always felt an education was important, as children should be taught as much as possible. Unfortunately, not all Amish feel that way. Some families are very strict and send their children to Amish schools only. Over all, our Amish schools are good; but, then, we do have some that have a share of problems with students and teachers.

Shelley: What might surprise others about the Amish?

J: That I don't think our way of life is hard at all. It is a blessed life, being close to nature, which God created. God is good.

Others might be surprised that not many people in some communities are farmers. We have a lot of woodshops, sawmills, welding shops, grocery bulk-food stores, variety stores (like Walmart), too. We also have sewing shops and fabric stores. All are owned and managed by Amish.

Also, if you want, you can buy all your Amish clothes. You don't have to make them. We also like to shop at Walmart and Aldi. Also Kohls!

Something else some might find surprising is that we would pay a driver to take us on vacation. A lot of Amish own houses in Sarasota, Florida, and will spend the winter months there.

And some Amish youth, when they turn eighteen, will sometimes buy a car and drive, but most time will sell the car after a time and become a member of the church. Most parents do not approve but will allow the child to stay at home with the family. There are some (few) parents who will not allow their child to stay at home if they have a car.

Shelley: Thank you both so much for doing this interview with me! I loved learning more about you and your families. I think my readers will enjoy learning more about the Amish, too.

Questions for Discussion

1. What is your first impression of Hannah? How might you have reacted to receiving such an envelope? What did you think about her family's decision to move?

2. Have you ever moved to a brand-new area like Hannah and her family did? What were some of the things you found different? How did you adjust?

3. Isaac Troyer's life changed after he survived a terrible illness. Why do you think it often takes a major event like that to appreciate each moment a little more?

4. The Hilty and Troyer families couldn't be more different. Who, besides Isaac and Hannah, do you think you are going to be able to connect with?

5. Had you heard of an Amish benefit auction before? What about a sandwich sale? Have you ever participated in any event like these? What were they like?

6. A lot of people in the Hilty family have been harboring secrets. How does each secret and its revelation change the family dynamics?

7. What did you think about Jenny Hilty's growth? What do you think will happen to her in the future?

8. Below is the scripture verse from James that guided me during the writing of the novel. What does it mean to you?

   How do you know what your life will be like tomorrow? Your life is like the morning fog—it's here a little while, then it's gone. James 4:14

9. Below is this book's Amish Proverb. Which character in the book do you think could use this good advice?

   Rare indeed is the person who looks for trouble and fails to find it. Amish Proverb

Facts About Hart County

1. Hart County is located in the middle of Kentucky Cave Country. Mammoth Cave National Park is located in this region, as well as a number of lesser-known caverns, many of which are open to the public.

2. A Civil War battle took place in Hart County. The Battle for the Bridge took place right along US Highway 31. The bridge in question was the L&N Railroad Bridge. A technical marvel for its time, it was almost 1,200 feet long and was 125 feet tall.

3. When driving around Hart County, be sure to look for the fifty painted quilts on the barns. The Barn Quilt Trail is a popular tourist activity.

4. There are all kinds of stories about how Horse Cave, Kentucky, got its name. Some say the name came from Native Americans. Others say that it was named because outlaws liked to hide their horses in the cavern. The town of Horse Cave was built over the cave, and the entrance is located in the middle of Main Street.

5. The Amish came to this area in the 1970s. Kentucky has the fastest growing Amish population in the United States.

6. The area is located about two hours from Louisville, KY, and two hours from Nashville, TN.

Center Point Large Print
600 Brooks Road / PO Box 1
Thorndike, ME 04986-0001 USA

(207) 568-3717

US & Canada:
1 800 929-9108
www.centerpointlargeprint.com